Eat·Your·Dessert Or·You·Won't·Get Any·Broccoli

Recipes of the families and friends of the
Sea Pines Montessori School
Hilton Head Island, South Carolina

Sea Pines
MONTESSORI SCHOOL

The recipes collected in "Eat Your Dessert or You Won't Get Any Broccoli", have been submitted by the families and friends of the Sea Pines Montessori School. The information contained in this book is true to the best of our knowledge. Some recipes are original creations and family traditions, others have been adapted from other sources. The authors and publisher disclaim all liability in connection with the use of this information.

First Printing September 1996   5,000

Copyright 1996

ISBN 0-9652637

Additional copies of this book may be obtained by sending
$16.95 per book plus
$3.00 postage and handling
(South Carolina residents add an additional .85¢) to:

Eat Your Dessert...
The Sea Pines Montessori School
9 Fox Grape Road
Hilton Head Island,
SC 29928

All proceeds from the sale of this book will enrich the programs at the Sea Pines Montessori School, a non-profit organization.

Printed in the United States of America
TOOF COOKBOOK DIVISION

STARR ★ TOOF

670 South Cooper Street
Memphis, TN 38104

TABLE OF CONTENTS

DEDICATION

Eat Your Dessert Or You Won't Get Any Broccoli is lovingly dedicated to our headmistress, Maxine M. Swingle and the children, past, present and future of the Sea Pines Montessori School.

Special thanks to: Lori Parker, who jumped in with both feet... Jacob Ranney, without his love of broccoli we'd still be searching for a title...Shelby Garner, who saw us through to...well, this! A debt of gratitude to the Anderson Group, who once again offered their valuable services in our time of need. And to Lynne Anderson, who always believed in us.

It was our goal to compile a collection of recipes that reflect our Montessori family, and the community of Hilton Head Island and the surrounding Lowcountry. We appreciate the enthusiasm and support of our friends, and families, (especially Steve and Steve). Thanks for the encouragement to all who encountered us during the crazy period between the concept and the sight of the UPS man pulling up to the school, boxes of books in tow.

– Lauren and Patte

ABOUT THE
SEA PINES MONTESSORI SCHOOL

The Sea Pines Montessori School is a non-profit preschool, founded in 1968 by Mary Fraser, wife of Charles Fraser, Sea Pines Plantation Developer. The Sea Pines Montessori School now enrolls close to 300 children, some of whom are children of alumni. The growth and success of the school is due to the fine staff of teachers and the active and productive support of the parents and community.

The goal of the school is to prepare the child for life, with the focus on the most vital stage of the child's life - the beginning. The program provides the foundation for a lifetime of the love of learning which develops the whole child - academically, physically, psychologically, socially and spiritually. This brings to fruition the potential of the child and develops the habits, skills, and positive attitudes that will remain with him throughout his life.

Cited by the Ford Foundation as one of the top preschools in the country, the Sea Pines Montessori School has achieved standards of excellence rarely found in preschools today. The curriculum centers around practical life skills, language development, refinement of the senses, mathematics, geography, history, geometry, science, botany, art, music, foreign language, drama and dance. Now as in the past, many families move to the Hilton Head area so that their children may attend. In addition, the Sea Pines Montessori School serves as a model for many schools around the country. The heart of the program lies in the respect for, faith in, and love of the child; the hope for a better tomorrow through the child of today.

"The most important period of life...is the first one, the period from birth to age six."
                                                                    -Dr. Maria Montessori

"Free the child's potential and you will transform him and the world."
                                                                    -Dr. Maria Montessori

EAT YOUR DESSERT COMMITTEE

We express our deep appreciation to the families and friends who generously contributed their favorite recipes. Unfortunately, due to our cost limitations and similarity of recipes, we were unable to publish all recipes received. We hope our friends will understand this compromise and share in our excitement for the finished product Eat Your Dessert or You Won't Get Any Broccoli.

CONTRIBUTORS

Carla Alagna
Carolyn Alford
Lea Allen
Lynne Anderson
Natalie Anderson
Nancy Balint
Luella Bauer
Karen Beall
Cindy Bell
Steve Boney
Anne Bradley
Melissa Bragg
Kerrie Brien
Cindy Brook
Elaine Brosman
Christina Bruderer
Patsy Cahill
Jennifer Cauble
Robin Cavella
Lenora Cheney
Donna Chupurdy
Carrie Collins
Sandra Couch
Kati Courtemanche
Gail Daunt
Robin DeRose
Rick Dextraze
Sunny DeZeeuw
Sharon Dimmock
Chrissy Du Rant
Mary K. Du Rant
Angela Ellis
Phyllis Ellison
Robin Ernest
Connie Everett
Debbie Fraser
Marilyn Fraser
Anuska Frey
Anna Fuller
Teri Fulton
Donna Gaal

Libby Galloway
Andrea Gannon
Al Garrett
Leslie Gintz
Suzanne Hawkins
Helen Haygood
Robin Hellman
Claudia Herrera
Lisa Hutto
Julie Jilly
Lui Kaiser
Carrie Kampermann
Carey Ann Kelley
Abbie Kelly
Ann Kieffer
Meredith Kronz
Jill La Force
Colleen Langley
Tanner Larson
Beverly Lauderdale
Cindi Lauderdale
Nancy Lauderdale
Dahris Lawrence
Marcy Lindgren
Mc Brier Maloney
Lauren Marlis
Agnes Marie Maroshek
Risa McMillan
Laurie Meccariello
Lorane Meredith
Ron Mildh
Lottie Anne Munday
Mary Frances Munday
Debbie Natoli
Meg O'Brien
Susie Oliver
Jennifer Olsen
Cathy Onorato
Lori Parker
Polly Patel
Jacki Pauls

Andrea Pejeau
Ann Piercy
Diane Prescott
Francie Puntereri
Joni Quigley
MJ Corcoran Rankin
Patte Ranney
Jody Reichel
Camille Renato
Leslie Richardson
Lois Richardson
Debi Rosica
Terry Roth
Gregg Russell
Linda Russell
Karen Ryan
Pat Savarese
Jane Schooler
Barb Schwitters
Gayle Shaffer
Jenny Slede
Beth Soby
Carolyn Sonberg
K-Kay Sonberg
Tom Stevens
Shannon Stratton
Joan Stuckart
Buzzy Sullivan
Sandy Sullivan
Larry Swingle
Maxine Swingle
Gayle Taylor
Jill Torre
Karen Tremarelli
Myra Truluck
Michele Vrettas
Lea Wade
Bunny Wallach
Arlene Williams
Melodie Williams
Cheryl Wilson

RESTAURANT CONTRIBUTORS

ALEXANDER'S
AUNT CHILADA'S
THE BEAUFORT INN
BESS' DELICATESSEN
BETSY'S GOURMET TO GO
BOAT HOUSE GRILL
CAFE AT BELFAIR
CAFE EUROPA
CAPTAIN'S SEAFOOD
CAROLINA CAFE AT THE WESTIN RESORT HILTON HEAD
CHARLIE'S L'ETOILLE VERTE
CQ'S
CRAZY CRAB
CROWNE PLAZA RESORT HILTON HEAD
FRATELLO'S
GIUSEPPI'S
GIUSEPPI'S PIZZA AND PASTA
HARBOURMASTER'S
HARBOURTOWN DELI
HEMINGWAY'S AT THE HYATT REGENCY HILTON HEAD
HILTON HEAD BREWING COMPANY
HOFBRAUHAUS
HUDSON'S
JULEP'S
THE KINGFISHER
LAND'S END TAVERN
LA POLA'S
OLD FORT PUB
OLD OYSTER FACTORY
PRIMO
REILLEY'S
RICK'S PLACE
SANTA FE CAFE
SCOTT'S FISH MARKET
SIGLER'S ROTISSERIE "THE CHEF'S PLACE"
SOUTH CAROLINA YACHT CLUB
STELLINI
TRUFFLES
TWO ELEVEN PARK

APPETIZERS

APPETIZERS

ENDIVE STUFFED WITH GOAT CHEESE & GRAPES

24 Belgian endive leaves, all one size
12 ounces goat cheese
1/4 cup capers
2 tablespoons extra virgin olive oil

8 slices crisp-cooked bacon, crumbled
30-40 seedless red grapes, halved
carrot curls

In a bowl, mash cheese until creamy. Stir in capers, oil and bacon. Spoon mixture into endive leaves and top with halved red grapes. Chill until ready to serve. Place stuffed leaves in a circle on a round platter to resemble a flower. Pile carrot curls in the center of the platter.

BACON-ASPARAGUS ROLLUPS

1 8-ounce package cream cheese, softened
6 slices crisp-cooked bacon, crumbled
1 tablespoon fresh chopped chives
1 cup mayonnaise

1 loaf white bread, crusts removed
1 bunch fresh asparagus spears or 1 15-ounce can asparagus, drained
1/4 cup butter, melted

Preheat oven to 400°. If using fresh asparagus, barely steam and then blanch in cold water; drain. In a medium size mixing bowl, combine cream cheese, bacon, chives and mayonnaise. Beat at medium speed one minute. Spread mixture on each slice of bread. Roll 2 asparagus spears in each slice of bread and cut into 3 bite-size rolls. Arrange on greased cookie sheet, putting seam side down and brush with melted butter. Bake for 12 minutes. May be prepared ahead and frozen.

Che'vre cheese (pronounced SHEHV-ruh and French for "goat"), is a moist, creamy, pure white goat's milk cheese with a pleasingly tart flavor that lends itself to many dishes.

This recipe is a favorite in December because it resembles a poinsettia on the plate.

SUPERB HOT SPINACH DIP

1 10-ounce package frozen spinach, thaw and squeeze dry
1 8-ounce package cream cheese, softened
1/3 cup half and half or heavy whipping cream

2 cups grated Monterey Jack cheese
3/4 cup chopped onions
1 tablespoon seeded and chopped jalapeño peppers
2 tomatoes, seeded, chopped

Preheat oven to 400°. Mix all ingredients together and pour into greased 1 1/2 quart dish. Bake for 20 - 25 minutes. Serve with crackers, chips, or crusty baguette slices.

GRILLED PORTABELLA MUSHROOMS

Food for thought: the portabella is actually the fully mature form of the more commonly known cremino mushroom.

1 pound portabella mushrooms (well rinsed)
1/2 cup extra virgin olive oil
1/2 cup balsamic vinegar

2 tablespoons fresh chopped parsley (or basil)
fresh cracked pepper
Jane's Krazy mixed up salt

Cut off the stems of the mushrooms leaving approximately 1/4" of the stem intact. Cut uniform 1/4" slices. Mix the rest of the ingredients in a bowl using salt and pepper to your liking. Completely coat the mushroom slices with the marinade in a shallow dish; cover and marinate in refrigerator 30 minutes prior to grilling. Sear on hot grill approximately 2 minutes on each side. *Yum, Yum, Yum!!! These also make a great side dish with grilled meats and fish.*

ARTICHOKE NIBBLES

2 6-ounce jars marinated
  artichoke hearts
1 small onion, finely chopped
1 garlic clove, minced
4 eggs beaten
1/4 cup fine breadcrumbs
1/4 teaspoon salt

1/8 teaspoon pepper
1/8 teaspoon oregano
dash of Tabasco sauce
2 cups grated sharp cheddar
  cheese
2 tablespoons chopped parsley

Preheat oven to 325°. Drain marinade from one jar of artichoke hearts into medium skillet. Drain second jar and discard marinade. Chop artichoke hearts and set aside. Heat marinade, add onions and garlic and sauté until onion is limp, about 5 minutes. In a large mixing bowl, combine eggs, breadcrumbs, salt, pepper, oregano and Tabasco. Fold in cheese and parsley. Add artichoke hearts and sautéed onion. Mix, blending well. Pour into 9" square glass baking dish. Bake 30 minutes, until top is golden brown. Allow to cool briefly before cutting into 1" squares.

TERRINE OF ARTICHOKE & CHEESES

2 6-ounce jars marinated
  artichoke hearts
1 medium onion
4 large eggs
2 egg yolks

6 ounces sharp cheddar
  cheese, grated
2 ounces Parmesan cheese,
  grated
1 1/2 teaspoons black pepper
generous pinch nutmeg

Preheat oven to 375°. Drain artichoke hearts, using marinade to sautéed onions. Chop artichoke hearts and set aside. Sauté onions until soft and somewhat translucent. Add artichoke hearts and sauté very briefly. In a mixing bowl, beat eggs and yolks together thoroughly. Combine eggs with cheeses, pepper and nutmeg and mix well.

Pour half of egg and cheese batter into a loaf pan. Gently spoon onion/artichoke mixture down the center of egg batter. Pour remaining egg and cheese batter over the top. Bake until top is very brown and toothpick inserted in center comes out clean, about 45 minutes to 1 hour. Cool in pan for half hour, then scrape around sides, invert onto board. Slice and enjoy.

FOOLPROOF ARTICHOKE DIP

1 cup mayonnaise
1 cup Parmesan cheese

1 6-ounce jar marinated
 artichoke hearts

Preheat oven to 350°. In an ovenproof bowl/dish combine the mayonnaise and cheese. Drain and chop artichokes and add to the mayonnaise mixture. Bake for 20-30 minutes.

COLD VEGGIE PIZZA SQUARES

2 packages Pillsbury crescent
 rolls
2 8-ounce packages cream
 cheese, softened
1 cup mayonnaise or Miracle
 Whip

2 envelopes ranch dressing
 mix
fresh broccoli and zucchini,
 chopped
carrots, grated

"The world of tomorrow walks on the feet of the children of today."
— Maria Montessori

Preheat oven to 350°. Roll out and pat crescent roll dough onto an ungreased cookie sheet. Bake for 10 minutes. Remove from oven and allow to cool. Mix the softened cream cheese, mayonnaise, and ranch dressing mix and spread onto cooled dough. Place the vegetables on top. Cut into squares, serve and enjoy!

GREEN PEPPER MUSTARD DIP

1 cup mayonnaise
1/4 cup Dijon style mustard
1 small garlic clove, peeled
 and chopped

1 teaspoon water-packed
 green peppercorns, drained
whole peppercorns

Combine all ingredients (except additional peppercorns), puree until smooth. Taste and correct seasoning, stir in additional peppercorns to taste. Do not process further. Cover and refrigerate until serving.

BENEDICTINE DIP

A Kentucky Derby favorite

---

1 large cucumber, peeled
1 medium onion
8 ounces cream cheese,
   softened
1/4 cup mayonnaise or more,
   to taste
seasoning salt
drop of green food coloring

In a food processor, grind the cucumber and onion, remove to strainer and bowl and drain overnight. The next day, in a medium bowl add the cream cheese to the cucumber and onion mixture, stir, add mayonnaise to desired consistency. Season to taste with seasoning salt. It is optional to add the food coloring but it does make it a pretty cucumber color. Serve with your favorite crackers or bagel chips.

CATFISH'S CRAB DIP

6 ounces crabmeat (cooked
   and cleaned or canned)
1/2 cup mayonnaise
8 ounces cream cheese
4 ounces grated cheddar
   cheese
garlic salt to taste
1 teaspoon Worcestershire
red pepper to taste

Mix all ingredients thoroughly in food processor. Chill and serve with crackers.

Absolutely no relation to the famous Benedictine monks in France, nor their sweet cognac-based liquor.
It is a tasty specialty, however, from Louisville, Kentucky and named after its creator, a local caterer.

COLIGNY CRAB MOLD OR DIP

1 package unflavored gelatin
3 tablespoons cold water
1 10½-ounce can regular
   cream of mushroom soup
6 ounces cream cheese at
   room temperature

8 ounces canned King Crab
1 cup chopped celery
1 green onion, chopped
1 cup mayonnaise

Dissolve gelatin in water. Set aside. In saucepan, heat soup, add gelatin and cool. Add cream cheese and beat until smooth. Stir in remaining ingredients. Pour into serving bowl or mold. Best if prepared 2 days ahead. Serve with pieces of sourdough bread or corn chips.

DIJON ARTICHOKE CRAB DIP

6 ounces crab meat, cleaned
   thoroughly
1 6-ounce jar marinated
   artichoke hearts, drained
   & chopped
1 8-ounce package cream
   cheese
2 tablespoons chopped green
   onions

2 tablespoons sour cream
2 teaspoons Dijon mustard
2 teaspoons fresh parsley
1 teaspoon lemon juice
½ teaspoon garlic powder
¼ teaspoon pepper

Microwave the cream cheese for about 1 minute, until soft. Stir in all remaining ingredients blending thoroughly. Cover loosely with waxed paper and microwave 3-4 minutes, stirring twice, until dip is heated through and just beginning to bulge around the edges. Serve with crackers or vegetables.

Blue crab is the crustacean of choice in most Lowcountry crab recipes. Found in abundance along the Carolina coast, these 10-legged saltwater scavengers boast blue claws and oval, dark blue-green shells that turn bright orange after only a couple minutes in a steamer. The meat is sweet and succulent. You can also purchase canned blue crabmeat, in most Lowcountry markets.

HOT CLAM & DILL APPETIZER

1 8-ounce package cream cheese, softened	2 tablespoons milk
1 8-ounce can of clams, drained	1/2 teaspoon cream style horseradish
2 tablespoons finely chopped onion	1/2 teaspoon salt
	dash of pepper
	sprinkle of dill

Preheat oven to 375°. Combine cream cheese, clams, onion, milk, horseradish and seasonings, mixing until well blended. Spoon into 9" pie plate or oven-proof dish; sprinkle with dill. Bake for 15 minutes. Serve as a dip or spread with crackers, chips or raw vegetables.

Variation: A 7¹/₂-ounce can of flaked, drained crabmeat and 1/2 cup sliced toasted almonds are excellent alternatives for the clams and dill.

CALIBOGUE CRAB CAKES

2 eggs	1 teaspoon sherry
1 small onion, diced	1 teaspoon Worcestershire
1 pound crab, picked over well	2/3 cup crushed saltines
1 tablespoon mayonnaise	1/4 to 1/2 teaspoon salt
	1/8 to 1/4 teaspoon pepper

Mix all ingredients and shape into crab cakes. Sauté in hot oil on both sides. Serve immediately.

Live clams can be found in the Lowcountry at low tide, nestled in the mud along saltwater inlets, some beaches and on many local riverbanks. Look for tiny holes spouting small water bubbles. Harvested mainly April through November, our local varieties are delicious simply steamed open and dipped in butter!

GREEN ONION SHRIMP DIP

1 cup finely chopped, peeled
and deveined cooked shrimp
1 8-ounce package cream
cheese, softened
1/2 cup finely chopped green
onion (white & green parts)

1 tablespoon chili sauce
1 1/2 teaspoon Tabasco
1/2 teaspoon salt
1/4 teaspoon white pepper
1/8 teaspoon paprika

Blend all ingredients. Cover and chill several hours. Serve as a
spread, dip or filling for celery, cherry tomatoes or endive
leaves.

CRESCENT SHRIMP ROLLS

1/2 pound shrimp, cooked and
chopped
1/2 teaspoon lemon juice
dab of horseradish
1 8-ounce package cream
cheese, softened

1/2 teaspoon chopped onion
mayonnaise to taste
1 package unbaked crescent
rolls

Mix all ingredients except crescent rolls and refrigerate
overnight. To prepare: cut rolls in half, spread with shrimp
mixture. Roll up and bake as directed on crescent roll package. *Fabulous.*

SHRIMP PÂTÉ

1 pound shrimp, boiled,
deveined and peeled
1 tablespoon mayonnaise
salt and pepper to taste

pinch of mace
5 drops Worcestershire sauce
Sherry to taste

In a blender or food processor with steel blade, combine all
ingredients until mixture is spreading consistency. Refrigerate.
Serve as spread with crackers, breads or on sandwiches.

MUSHROOM CHICKEN LIVER PÂTÉ

1 pound chicken livers	**1/2 cup white table wine**
1/2 pound fresh mushrooms	**3 drops Tabasco**
1/4 cup butter	**1/2 cup butter, softened**
1 teaspoon garlic salt	**dash salt**
1 teaspoon paprika	**fresh parsley**
1/3 cup green onions, chopped	

Sauté livers, mushrooms, garlic salt, paprika and onion in 1/4 cup butter for 5 minutes. Add wine and Tabasco; cover and cook slowly, 5-10 minutes. Cool; whirl in blender, blend in 1/2 cup softened butter and salt to taste. Turn into dish; chill overnight. Unmold, garnish with parsley.

CURRIED CHICKEN BALLS

Makes 20 small appetizers

1-2 boneless chicken breasts,	**1 teaspoon curry**
cooked and cooled	**dash salt**
2 tablespoons Major Grey's	**mayonnaise**
chopped chutney	**chopped almonds**

Cut the chicken into small chunks. Blend together the chicken, chutney, curry and salt. Add enough mayonnaise to make the mixture moist. Shape the balls and roll in chopped almonds. Chill.

SAUSAGE BITES

1 pound sausage, hot or mild	**2 cups grated sharp cheddar**
3 cups Bisquick mix	**cheese**
	1/3 cup milk

Preheat oven to 325°. Brown sausage, drain grease and crumble sausage. Mix Bisquick, milk, cheese and sausage. Knead thoroughly. Roll into little balls. Bake until brown. Serve immediately.

MINI PIZZA APPETIZERS

1 pound ground chuck	2 teaspoons basil
1 pound Italian sausage	1/2 onion chopped (optional)
1 pound grated cheddar cheese	1 tablespoon fennel seeds
	1 teaspoon garlic salt
2 teaspoons oregano	1 to 2 loaves cocktail rye

Brown the ground chuck, sausage and onions. Drain off the fat. Add the cheese and remaining ingredients (except rye bread) stirring until cheese is melted. Spread mixture on bread slices. Place on cookie sheets. Bake at 350° for 10 minutes or until hot and bubbly.

Freezes well; place frozen appetizers on cookie sheet and bake at 400° for 10 minutes or until hot and bubbly.

Let the children help with this easy pizza appetizer. It's assembly line style preparation lends itself to both their technical skills and taste buds.

POLLY'S FAMOUS SALSA WITH BLACK BEANS

1 19-ounce can cannellini beans, not drained (white kidney beans)	1 10-ounce tomato salsa
	1 teaspoon ground cumin
	1 teaspoon basil
2 15 1/2-ounce cans black beans, drained	1/2 teaspoon oregano
	2-3 cloves garlic, chopped

Mix all ingredients together and heat in microwave on high 10 minutes, stir, and heat 20 minutes more on medium low. Stir again. Serve as a dip with grated cheese or over cooked rice with grated cheese and onions.

BONITA TEX-MEX DIP

3 medium ripe avocados
2 tablespoons lemon juice
1/2 teaspoon salt
1/4 teaspoon pepper
1 cup sour cream
1/2 cup mayonnaise
1 package taco seasoning mix
2 10 1/2-ounce cans plain or
   jalapeño bean dip
1 cup chopped green onions

3 medium size ripe tomatoes,
   halved, seeded, coarsely
   chopped
2 3 1/2-ounce cans pitted
   black olives, drained and
   coarsely chopped
2 cups grated sharp cheddar
   cheese
large round tortilla chips

Peel, pit and mash avocados with lemon juice, salt and pepper. In another bowl combine sour cream, mayonnaise and taco seasoning. To assemble, spread bean dip on a large shallow serving platter, top with seasoned avocado, layer with sour cream taco mixture. Sprinkle with chopped onions, tomatoes and olives, cover with grated cheese. Serve chilled or at room temperature with chips.

GOOD & EASY GUACAMOLE

2 large ripe avocados
1/3 teaspoon garlic powder
juice of one lemon
1/2 cup salsa, the kind made in
   Texas, thick and chunky
   salsa (medium hot)

fresh cilantro
fresh parsley
blue corn chips

Peel, pit and mash avocados but not completely, leaving some chunks in. Add garlic powder and the lemon juice. Fold in the salsa and fresh minced cilantro, a little cilantro goes a long way, add fresh minced parsley. Serve with blue corn chips.

*Food for thought:
Always place the
avocado pit in
guacamole or
cold avocado
soup to prevent
discoloration.
Remove the pit
at serving time.
If using only part
of an avocado,
leave the pit in
the remaining
unused part.*

*For purists,
substitute for the
salsa: one large
tomato diced,
one medium
onion diced,
3 - 4 fresh
chopped garlic
cloves and
chopped fresh
cilantro to taste.
Add salt &
pepper.*

CALIENTE SALSA

4 28-ounce cans crushed
  tomatoes
2 4-ounce cans chopped
  green chilies
1 4-ounce can chopped
  jalapeños
1 large green pepper, chopped
2 medium onions, chopped

1/4 cup lemon juice
6 tablespoons white vinegar
1 tablespoon oregano
2 tablespoons sugar
1 tablespoon garlic salt
1 1/2 teaspoons ground cumin
2 teaspoons chili powder

In a large saucepan combine all ingredients and bring to a boil. Simmer for 5 minutes. Remove from heat and allow to cool. Refrigerate in airtight container.

RANCH PRETZELS

"Young children have a strong, natural ability to concentrate."
— Maria Montessori

1 pound Dutch style pretzels
1 envelope ranch dressing mix
1 cup oil

1 teaspoon garlic powder
1 teaspoon dill weed
1 teaspoon lemon pepper

Preheat oven to 300°. Break pretzels into pieces. Combine ranch dressing mix, oil, garlic powder, dill weed, lemon pepper. Put pretzel pieces in bottom section of broiler pan, pour dressing mixture over, stir to coat. Bake 10 minutes, stir, bake another 10 minutes.

SEASONED OYSTER CRACKERS

1 envelope ranch dressing mix
1 teaspoon garlic powder
1 teaspoon dill weed

2/3 cup corn oil
1 package oyster crackers

Shake together in bag or tupperware container ranch dressing mix, garlic powder and dill weed. Add oyster crackers to seasonings, shake again. Add oil to seasoned crackers.
Shake again, turning over several times. Leave overnight.
For less oily crackers, after mixing, put crackers in paper bag.

BENNE STICKS

1/3 cup sesame seeds
1 cup flour
cayenne pepper to taste
3 tablespoons butter

3 tablespoons solid Crisco
   shortening
2/3 tablespoon ice water

Preheat oven to 300°. Bake sesame seeds in oven until golden brown, about 15 minutes. In a mixing bowl combine flour, pepper, butter and shortening with pastry blender until mixture looks like coarse meal. Add sesame seeds and while stirring with a fork add 2/3 tablespoon ice water to form dough. Roll dough into a rectangle 1/8" thick. Cut into desired lengths. Place on baking sheet. Bake at 325° for 15 minutes or until golden.

CHEESE BUTTONS

1 cup margarine
2 cups grated sharp cheddar
   cheese

2 cups flour
2 cups Rice Krispies cereal

Preheat oven to 325°. Soften margarine to room temperature. Combine with other ingredients, mixing thoroughly. Roll into small balls then place on an ungreased cookie sheet and flatten with a fork. Bake until light tan, about 18 minutes. *One recipe makes 100 or more buttons.*

LIGHT HERBED CHEESE DIP

1 8-ounce light cream cheese,
   room temperature
1/4 cup plain nonfat yogurt
2 teaspoons each chopped
   dill and parsley

2 scallions, thinly sliced
2 cloves garlic, minced
salt and pepper to taste

Puree yogurt and cream cheese in food processor until smooth. Add rest of ingredients, puree until blended. Serve as a dip for veggies. *9 calories per tablespoon.*

Benne seeds, or sesame seeds, were first brought to America by African slaves and have been popular in Southern cooking ever since. This cocktail wafer is linked to the culture of Charleston, South Carolina, where you'll find proprietors serving several different benne seed products along the open air markets in historic downtown, Charleston.

BRIE EN CROUTE

1 egg yolk
8" wheel of brie

1 Pepperidge Farm frozen
puff pastry sheet

Preheat oven to 375°. Beat egg yolk with 1 teaspoon water. Thaw one sheet of puff pastry 20 minutes, then unfold. Roll out large enough to cover top and side of the wheel of brie. Cover brie with pastry and place in quiche dish. Brush top of pastry with egg mixture. If desired, decorate with cutouts made from pastry scraps and apply with egg mixture. Brush the cutouts with egg. Place in the middle of oven. Bake for 15-20 minutes or until golden brown. For a variation, top with almonds, raspberry preserves or both the last 5 minutes of baking. Serve with crackers.

JALAPEÑO JELLY DIP

8 ounces grated cheddar
cheese
1 cup chopped pecans,
toasted

3 or 4 green onions, chopped
dash of Tabasco
mayonnaise
jalapeño jelly

Mix first 4 ingredients together. Add enough mayonnaise to make it stick together. Spread mixture on a large plate and top with jelly. Serve with crackers.

TUSCANY CHEESE SPREAD

3½ cups grated sharp
cheddar cheese
1 8-ounce can water chest-
nuts, drained, coarsely
chopped

1 cup mayonnaise
¼ cup chopped, drained, oil
packed sun-dried tomatoes
¼ teaspoon cayenne pepper

Preheat oven to 350°. Combine all ingredients in a large bowl and mix well. Transfer to a 1 quart baking dish. Bake until bubbly, 20-30 minutes. Serve with crackers or cocktail bread.

GOODA GOUDA CHEESE BALL

1 package crescent rolls   **spicy brown mustard**
1 round Gouda cheese

Preheat oven to 375°. Open the rolls and arrange them in a star pattern like figure #1. Spread with mustard. Remove wax from cheese and put cheese in the center of the star. Fold all the "points" over the cheese—mold the dough with your hands to make sure cheese is completely sealed. Place on greased cookie sheet and bake for 20 minutes, until deep golden brown. Serve with crackers and fresh fruit garnish.

figure #1

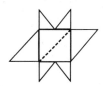

Clean little hands love to assemble this appetizer.... and love to devour it as well.

CHEESE FINGERS

1 cup all-purpose flour   **1/4 teaspoon cayenne pepper**
1 cup grated sharp cheddar   **1/4 cup butter**
   cheese   **1 egg, beaten**
3/4 teaspoon salt

Preheat oven to 425°. In a large bowl, mix together the flour, cheese, salt and cayenne pepper. Cut in the butter with fork until the mixture looks like corn meal. Add the beaten egg and stir. Knead until you can form a ball. If the dough seems dry, add a few drops of water. Place on a floured board and roll thin. Cut in finger-sized strips and place on a lightly greased cookie sheet. Bake until lightly browned, about 5-8 minutes.

SALMON MOUSSE

1 package unflavored gelatin
3 tablespoons lemon juice
$1/2$ cup boiling water
$1/2$ cup mayonnaise
2 cups cooked salmon or
   1 16-ounce can, drained

$1/4$ teaspoon paprika
1 teaspoon chopped dill
1 cup heavy cream
watercress for garnish
thin lemon slices for garnish

Combine the gelatin, lemon juice and boiling water in a blender and blend at high speed for 40 seconds. Add the mayonnaise, salmon, paprika and dill and blend briefly. Add cream while blending for 30 seconds or more. Pour into a 4 cup mold. Chill until mousse is set. Turn mold onto a serving platter. Garnish with watercress and lemon slices. Serve with crackers.

CUCUMBER MOUSSE

2 cucumbers, peeled and
   seeded
1 tablespoon lemon juice
2 tablespoons onion flakes
2 tablespoons boiling water
$1/2$ teaspoon pepper
1 teaspoon salt
1-2 tablespoons dill weed

3 envelopes (1/4 ounce)
   unflavored gelatin
$1/2$ cup cold water
$1/2$ cup mayonnaise
1 cup heavy cream
lettuce to garnish
cherry tomatoes to garnish

Using a metal blade in a food processor, chop and blend cucumber and lemon juice. Rehydrate onion flakes in boiling water, then add to cucumbers, blend in pepper, salt and dill weed. Soften gelatin in cold water. Add to cucumber mixture and process for 10 seconds. Add mayonnaise and process 5 seconds. Add cream and process until barely blended. Pour into a 5 cup ring mold which has been lightly greased with mayonnaise. Chill 2 hours or until firm. Unmold onto a bed of lettuce, and fill with cherry tomatoes. Serve with melba toasts.

BREAD & BREAKFAST

BREAD & BREAKFAST

✿ *BREAD MACHINE RECIPES*

ORANGE BLOSSOM CRANBERRY BREAD

1 egg
1 cup orange juice
1 cup sugar
1/4 cup melted shortening
3 cups all-purpose flour
4 teaspoons baking powder

1/2 teaspoon salt
1 1/2 teaspoons grated orange peel
1 cup chopped fresh cranberries
1/2 cup chopped walnuts

Preheat oven to 350°. Place egg, orange juice, sugar and shortening in bowl. Beat with electric mixer at moderate speed for 30 seconds. Scrape bowl. Combine flour, baking powder, salt and orange peel. Beating slowly, add flour mixture to egg mixture, mixing about 15 seconds. Stop and scrape bowl. Fold in cranberries and walnuts. Spread batter in greased 9 x 5 x 3" loaf pan. Bake for 55-60 minutes. Remove from pan and cool on wire rack. Also great as muffins. Bake regular sized muffins for approximately 40 - 45 minutes.

STRAWBERRY NUT BREAD

3 cups plain flour
1 teaspoon baking soda
1 teaspoon salt
3 teaspoons cinnamon
1 1/4 cups vegetable oil

2 cups sugar
3 well beaten eggs
2 10-ounce packages frozen strawberries, thawed
1 cup chopped nuts

Preheat oven to 350°. Mix ingredients until well moistened. Pour into 2 greased and floured 9 x 5 x 3" loaf pans. Bake for 1 hour. Check with a toothpick for doneness.

"The most important period of life is not the age of university studies but the period from birth to the age of six... for that is the time when intelligence itself, her greatest implement, is being formed..."
— Maria Montessori

BANANA TEA BREAD

2 cups granulated sugar	4 eggs, well beaten
1 cup butter	2¹/₂ cups sifted cake flour
6 ripe medium bananas, mashed	1 teaspoon salt
	2 teaspoons baking soda

Preheat oven to 350°. In a large bowl cream together the sugar and butter until fluffy. Add the bananas and eggs and blend. Sift together the flour, salt, and soda 3 times. Carefully blend the flour mixture into the banana mixture. Do not overmix. Pour the batter into 2 greased 9 x 5 x 3" loaf pans. Bake for 50-55 minutes or until a toothpick inserted in the middle comes out clean. Cool for 10 minutes. Remove the loaves from the pans and cool completely on racks before slicing. *Note: Loaves may be refrigerated, wrapped in foil, for 2 weeks or frozen for up to 3 months. The recipe may be halved for one loaf.*

The greatest happiness of life is the conviction that we are loved, loved for ourselves, or rather loved in spite of ourselves.

BANANA PECAN LOAF

3 very ripe bananas	1¹/₂ cups flour
¹/₂ cup Wesson oil	1 teaspoon baking soda
1¹/₂ cups sugar	¹/₃ cup sour cream
2 eggs, well beaten	¹/₂ cup chopped pecans
¹/₄ teaspoon salt	

Preheat oven to 350°. Peel and mash bananas, set aside. In a large mixing bowl, cream oil and sugar; add eggs and salt and mix well. Stir together the flour and soda, combine with sugar mixture alternating with sour cream. Add bananas and stir thoroughly. Fold in nuts. Grease 2 regular-sized loaf pans; pour in mixture and bake approximately 45 minutes. When bread leaves sides of pan and toothpick comes out clean, it is done. Cool in pans on racks for ¹/₂ hour, then remove bread from pans and allow to cool completely before slicing. Substitute ¹/₂ cup mini-chocolate chips for nuts ,or use nuts and chips.

AUTUMN PUMPKIN BREAD

2 eggs
1 1/2 cups sugar
1/2 cup oil
1 cup pumpkin (canned)
1/3 cup water
1 3/4 cups flour

1/4 teaspoon baking powder
1 teaspoon baking soda
1 teaspoon salt (optional)
1/2 teaspoon each of cloves, allspice, nutmeg and cinnamon

TOPPING:
1/3 cup brown sugar
1 teaspoon butter

1 teaspoon cinnamon

Preheat oven to 350°. In a large bowl, cream together eggs, sugar and oil. Add the pumpkin and water. In a separate bowl, sift together the flour, baking powder, baking soda, salt and spices. Stir into pumpkin mixture. Pour into greased 9 x 5 x 3" loaf pan. In a small bowl combine brown sugar, butter and cinnamon, dot on top of loaves. Bake approximately 1 hour. Recipe can be doubled in 2 loaf pans or 1 tube pan. Bake for 1 1/2 hours. *Freezes well.*

PUMPKIN, DATE & NUT LOAF

1 3/4 cups all-purpose flour
1 teaspoon baking soda
1/4 teaspoon salt
2/3 cup firmly packed brown sugar
1 1/4 teaspoon pumpkin pie spice

1 cup mashed, cooked pumpkin
1/3 cup orange juice
2 tablespoons vegetable oil
1 egg, beaten
1/3 cup chopped pitted dates
1/4 cup chopped walnuts

Preheat oven to 350°. Combine first 5 ingredients in large bowl and stir well. Make a well in center of mixture. In separate bowl combine pumpkin and next three ingredients. Add to dry ingredients. Stir just until dry ingredients are moistened (actually I do all of this with the mixer). Fold in dates and nuts. Spoon batter into an 8 1/2 x 4 1/2" loaf pan prepared with cooking spray. Bake for 60 minutes or until a toothpick inserted into the center comes out clean. Let cool for 10 minutes on wire rack and remove from pan. Let cool completely before slicing. *This bread has a great flavor and is a favorite with children too.*

BREAD

POPPYSEED BREAD

1 package Butter Pecan cake mix
1 package instant coconut pudding
4 eggs

½ cup oil
1 cup hot water
1 tablespoon poppyseeds
½ cup chopped pecans

Preheat oven 350°. Mix all ingredients. Pour into 2 large greased loaf pans or 5 small loaf pans. Bake for 1 hour. Check with toothpick for doneness.

ZUCCHINI BREAD

A deliciously different and decidedly easy version of this perennial favorite!

2 cups grated zucchini
3 eggs
1 cup oil
2 cups sugar
1 teaspoon vanilla
3 cups all-purpose flour
1 tablespoon cinnamon

1 teaspoon salt
1 teaspoon baking soda
1 teaspoon baking powder
1 cup raisins
1 cup chopped walnuts or pecans

Preheat oven to 350°. Grease 2 loaf pans. In a large mixing bowl, beat together the eggs, oil, sugar and vanilla. Sift together the flour, cinnamon, salt, soda and powder. Mix the dry ingredients with the wet ingredients, then add raisins and chopped nuts. Fold in the grated zucchini. Bake for 50-60 minutes, until a toothpick inserted in the center of loaf comes out clean. Refrigerates well.

LEMON-BLUEBERRY MUFFINS

1 3/4 cups all-purpose flour
1/2 cup plus 2 tablespoons
  sugar
2 teaspoons baking powder
1/4 teaspoon salt
1/2 cup chopped walnuts
  (optional)

1 teaspoon grated lemon peel
1 extra large egg
1 cup milk
4 tablespoons butter or
  margarine
1 teaspoon vanilla
1 1/2 cups blueberries

Preheat oven to 400°. Grease a 12 cup muffin tin or line tin
with cupcake papers. In a large bowl combine flour, sugar,
baking powder and salt. Stir in walnuts and lemon peel. In a
small bowl beat egg, milk, butter and vanilla. Pour egg mixture into dry ingredients and stir just until flour is moistened
(batter will be lumpy). Fold in blueberries. Spoon into muffin
cups and bake 20-22 minutes or until tops are golden. Makes
12 muffins.

STRAWBERRY YOGURT MUFFINS

2 cups all-purpose flour
1/2 cup sugar
1 1/2 teaspoons baking soda
1/2 teaspoon salt
2 eggs
1 cup plain low-fat yogurt

4 tablespoons melted butter
  or margarine
1 teaspoon vanilla
1 cup chopped fresh strawberries

Preheat oven to 375°. Grease a 12 cup muffin tin or line tin
with cupcake papers. In a large bowl combine flour, sugar,
baking soda and salt. In another bowl with spoon, beat
together eggs, yogurt, butter and vanilla until blended. Toss
strawberries with dry ingredients. Pour egg mixture into dry
ingredients and stir until flour is just moistened (batter will be
lumpy). Spoon into muffin cups. Bake 20-25 minutes or until
tops are golden. Makes 12 muffins.

PUMPKIN CHOCOLATE CHIP MUFFINS

$1^2/_3$ cups flour
1 cup sugar
1 tablespoon pumpkin pie
  spice
1 teaspoon baking soda
$^1/_4$ teaspoon baking powder
$^1/_4$ teaspoon salt

2 large eggs
1 cup canned pumpkin
$^1/_2$ cup butter, melted
1 cup chocolate chips
$^1/_2$ cup sliced almonds,
  unblanched

Preheat oven to 350°. Grease muffin cups or use paper liners. In a medium bowl mix flour, sugar, pie spice, baking soda, baking powder and salt. In a large bowl mix eggs, pumpkin and butter until blended. Add chocolate chips and almonds. Mix in dry ingredients, stir until well mixed. Pour batter into muffin cups $^1/_2$ - $^2/_3$ full. Bake 20-25 minutes.

If wrapped in plastic, bread will keep for one week. Flavor is even better the second day. Re-warm for 10 - 15 seconds in the microwave.

MORNING GLORY MUFFINS

4 cups all-purpose flour
$2^1/_2$ cups sugar
4 teaspoons baking soda
4 teaspoons cinnamon
1 teaspoon salt
4 cups peeled, grated apples
1 cup raisins

1 cup chopped pecans
1 cup shredded coconut
1 cup grated carrots
6 large eggs
1 cup vegetable oil
4 teaspoons vanilla

Preheat oven to 350°. Grease or paper line 36 muffin cups. In large bowl, sift flour, sugar, soda, cinnamon and salt. Stir in apples, raisins, pecans, coconut and carrots. Mix well. In blender, food processor or large bowl, combine eggs, oil and vanilla. Add to flour mixture and stir just until blended. Spoon batter into prepared muffin cups, filling $^2/_3$ full. Bake in pre-heated oven for 35 minutes or until muffins are springy to the touch. Let cool in pans on wire rack for 5 minutes, then remove from pans to rack to cool completely. Makes 36 muffins or 100 miniature muffins.

Muffins represent the ultimate comfort food. Homemade, warm, individual portions. Not as decadent as cookies— usually —but just as good! As delicious for breakfast as they are served in a basket at dinner.

Morning glory muffins are extravagant and worth every bit of the effort.

SIX WEEK BRAN MUFFINS

2 cups water	5 cups flour
5 teaspoons baking soda	cinnamon to taste
1 cup butter	nutmeg to taste
2 cups sugar	vanilla to taste
4 eggs	2 cups Bran Flakes or 4 cups
1 quart buttermilk	All-Bran

In a saucepan, boil water with baking soda for 30 seconds. Set aside and cool. In a separate bowl, cream together the butter and sugar and then add the eggs. Mix thoroughly. Next, alternately add the buttermilk and flour, mixing after each addition. Add seasonings as desired. Add the water mixture to the batter and mix thoroughly, blend in the bran cereal. Stir and refrigerate overnight. When ready to bake, stir and fill muffin cups. Bake at 375° for 30 minutes.

This muffin batter will keep in the refrigerator in an airtight container for up to six weeks. For fresh muffins every morning, simply stir once before filling muffin tins and bake.

CHOCOLATE CHIP MUFFINS

1¹/₂ cups all-purpose flour	1 cup chocolate chips
¹/₂ cup sugar	1 egg
3 teaspoons baking powder	1 cup milk
¹/₄ teaspoon salt	¹/₃ cup butter, melted

Preheat oven to 375°. Mix dry ingredients and add chocolate chips. In separate bowl, combine egg, milk and butter and stir into flour mixture. DO NOT BEAT. Pour in muffin tins. Bake for 20 minutes. A few melted chocolate chips drizzled over the top is a must for chocolate lovers.

Kids love to help make these.

CORN BREAD

1 box Jiffy corn bread mix
1 cup kernel corn
1 cup milk
1 egg, beaten

1/2 teaspoon salt
1 teaspoon grated onion
4 tablespoons butter, melted

Preheat oven to 350°. Mix all ingredients. Grease or butter a
9 x 13" pan. Bake for 55 minutes. Cool slightly. Cut into
squares. Serve warm.

JALAPEÑO CORN BREAD

1/2 cup butter
1/2 cup chopped onion
1 clove garlic, minced
1 roasted red pepper peeled,
    seeded and chopped
1-2 jalapeño peppers, finely
    chopped
1 cup whole corn kernels
1 1/2 cups yellow cornmeal

1 cup flour
1/2 cup sugar
1 tablespoon baking powder
1 teaspoon salt
1 1/2 cups buttermilk
2 eggs, slightly beaten
1 cup grated Monterey Jack
    cheese

Preheat oven 350°. Melt butter in a 10" cast-iron oven-proof
skillet over medium-low heat; sauté onion, garlic, red pepper,
jalapeños, and corn kernels until tender, about 5 minutes.

In a large bowl, sift together cornmeal, flour, sugar, baking
powder, and salt. Stir in buttermilk and eggs. Add sautéed mixture, stir until incorporated. Add cheese and stir.

Pour batter back into skillet; bake in oven for 30-35 minutes
until golden brown on the edges and firm to touch. Let the
corn bread sit for 20-30 minutes before cutting into wedges.

LUELLA'S SWEET WHEAT TOASTING BREAD

1 cup white flour	2 cups whole wheat flour
3 teaspoons baking powder	4 tablespoons melted
1 teaspoon salt	shortening
1 cup sugar	1¹/₂ cups milk

Preheat oven to 350°. Grease a loaf pan. In a mixing bowl, sift together white flour, baking powder, salt, and sugar. Stir in wheat flour, add melted shortening and milk. Pour in pan and bake for 1 hour. This bread makes excellent toast.

SALLY'S OLD-FASHIONED RYE BREAD

2 envelopes active dry yeast	1 tablespoon caraway seeds
2¹/₂ cups very warm water	crushed
¹/₄ cup light molasses	5¹/₂ - 6 cups sifted all-purpose
4 teaspoons salt	flour
2 tablespoons shortening	Cornmeal
2¹/₂ cups rye flour	

Sprinkle yeast into ¹/₂ cup of very warm water; stir in 1 teaspoon of molasses until yeast dissolves. Let stand, undisturbed, to proof until bubbly and double in volume, about 10 minutes. Combine remaining water and molasses with salt and shortening in a large bowl; stir in yeast mixture, rye flour and caraway seeds. Add enough all-purpose flour to make a soft dough. Turn out onto lightly floured surface. Knead until smooth and elastic, about 10 minutes, using enough of the remaining flour to keep dough from sticking. Place in buttered bowl, turn dough to bring buttered side up. Cover with towel. Let rise in a warm place, away from draft, 1 hour, or until double in bulk.

Butter large cookie sheet. Sprinkle lightly with cornmeal. Punch down dough, turn out onto lightly floured surface, knead a few times, invert bowl over dough, let rest 10 minutes. Divide dough in half. Knead each half a few times. Shape into 2 loaves. Place 4" apart on cookie sheet. Let rise again in warm place, away from draft, 45 minutes or until double in bulk. Brush tops with melted butter. Bake in hot oven 400° for 35 minutes or until browned and loaves sound hollow when tapped. Remove from cookie sheet to wire rack. Cool.

Sally Humphrey served as the first Headmistress of The Sea Pines Montessori School. A loved and respected educator, she was known too, for her work in the kitchen and especially her bread recipes. Her daughter, Jennifer, a teacher at the school shared some of her mother's recipes with us.

37

WHOLE WHEAT BREAD

1 package active dry yeast
1/2 cup lukewarm water
   (105° to 115°)
1 cup milk
1 cup boiling water
2 tablespoons shortening
2 tablespoons molasses,
   honey or sugar

2 teaspoons salt
3 cups unbleached flour
3 cups whole wheat flour
   (stone-ground)
1 tablespoon shortening for
   greasing bowl
1/8 cup gluten flour

Preheat oven to 375°. Sprinkle yeast over lukewarm water, stir. Let stand 5-10 minutes to proof. In a separate bowl, mix milk, boiling water, shortening, molasses and salt. Let cool to lukewarm and add to the yeast mixture. Wash, dry, and grease the second bowl and set aside. With a wooden spoon or mixer, gradually beat in unbleached flour 1 cup at a time. Then gradually beat in whole wheat flour. When dough becomes too stiff to beat, work in remaining flour by hand. You may not need to use entire amount. Knead, and let rise. When double in bulk, punch down. Grease two pans. Divide dough in two, and let rise again. Bake for 50 minutes.

ALLIGATOR BREAD
Bread Machine Recipe

Called Alligator Bread because it has "teeth," this hearty loaf is great for avocado, sprouts and tomato sandwiches.

1 1/4 cups water
3 tablespoons honey
2 tablespoons canola oil
2 tablespoons molasses
3 cups wheat bread flour
1 tablespoon gluten

1 tablespoon wheat germ
1/3 cup sunflower seeds
1/3 cup pumpkin seeds
2 1/2 teaspoons bread machine
   yeast

Place the first seven ingredients in bread pan, make a crater in the center and place the yeast there. Select "wheat" and a medium crust. If your machine does not have a wheat setting, be sure to include an extra knead. After the first knead; approximately 15 minutes, add the seeds. The bread takes about 4 hours to bake. Makes a 1 1/2 pound loaf. Note: Gluten gives the whole wheat the structure necessary for a good loaf. It can be found at health food stores.

CHOCOLATE CHIP BREAD
Bread Machine Recipe
Recipe for 1¹/₂ pound breadmakers that make round loaves.

1 package yeast
3 cups bread flour
2 tablespoons brown sugar
2 tablespoons granulated
  sugar
1 teaspoon salt
1 teaspoon cinnamon

4 tablespoons butter or
  margarine, softened
1 egg-very important at room
  temperature
1 cup warm milk
¹/₄ cup warm water
1 cup mini chocolate chips

In order listed, pour first 10 ingredients into bread pan. Select white bread setting and push start. When the Auto Bakery beeps- 5 minutes from end of second mixing, add the chocolate chips. Continue until finished. Tastes great warm but allow to cool a little before serving as chocolate chips may be hot.

CINNAMON CRANBERRY BREAD
Bread Machine Recipe

1¹/₄ cups water
2 tablespoons butter
3¹/₄ cups bread flour
¹/₄ cup sugar
1¹/₂ teaspoons salt

1 teaspoon ground cinnamon
3 teaspoons bread machine
  yeast
³/₄ cup dried cranberries

Place the first six ingredients in bread pan, as listed, making a crater in the center of the flour. Pour yeast into crater. Select "sweet" or "white" setting. Choose a light crust. After about 15 minutes add the cranberries. Bread is done in about 3 hours. This makes a 1¹/₂ pound loaf.

FRUIT BREAD
Bread Machine Recipe

Use any white bread machine recipe you like but especially one with eggs and sugar. A good one is this challah bread. Small individual sheets of dough are then wrapped around a nut and dried fruit mixture given below. For the bread: (add ingredients in the order called for by your machine instructions)

CHALLAH (EGG) BREAD:

3 cups white bread flour	2 eggs
2 tablespoons sugar	1 egg yolk
1 1/2 teaspoons salt	2 teaspoons active dry yeast
1/4 cup unsalted butter	3/4 cup water

Set your machine to produce dough only (no baking). While the machine is doing the hard work, make the nut and fruit mixture described below. Dump the finished dough (it will be sticky) on a floured surface, lightly flour the top as necessary and roll out to very thin - about 1/4". It will be at least 3 times as thick in the finished bread and with wrapping, you'll have 2 or 3 layers in each individual loaf. Cut into 3-4" squares or experiment with other shapes. Place a heaping forkful or so of the filling on each piece and close by pasting edges with water from a pastry brush. If some filling sticks out, as in a cornucopia, it will be okay. Bake at 350° for 20-25 minutes.

Food for thought: Challah is a traditional Jewish yeast bread. It has a light, airy texture

FILLING:

1/4 cup brown sugar	1 teaspoon coriander
1/2 cup almond paste	1 cup dried apples diced
3 1/2 tablespoons butter	1/2 cup pecan pieces (optional)

Of great benefit is to microwave this mixture for 30 seconds on high before thoroughly mixing.

WHEAT & HONEY BREAD
Bread Machine Recipe
Recipe for 1¹/₂ pound breadmakers that make round loaves.

1 package yeast
³/₄ cup whole wheat flour
2¹/₂ cups bread flour
1 teaspoon salt
2 tablespoons butter or margarine

1 egg room, temperature
1 cup plus 1 tablespoon warm water
2 tablespoons honey

In order listed, put all ingredients into bread pan, select white bread and push start. Make sure you add the honey last. This is delicious as toast.

OATMEAL BREAD
Bread Machine Recipe

1 cup water
¹/₄ cup molasses
2 tablespoons butter
3 cups bread flour
¹/₂ cup quick cooking or regular oats

2 tablespoons dry milk
1¹/₄ teaspoons salt
2¹/₂ teaspoons bread machine yeast

Place ingredients in bread pan in order listed. Select sweet setting and let her cook.

HERB GARLIC BREAD

Bread Machine Recipe

1¹/₄ cups water
1 tablespoon butter
2 cloves garlic, crushed
3¹/₄ cups bread flour
2 tablespoons sugar
1¹/₂ teaspoons salt

¹/₂ teaspoon dried rosemary
¹/₄ teaspoon dried thyme
¹/₄ teaspoon dried basil
2¹/₂ teaspoons bread machine yeast

Place all ingredients in bread pan in order listed. Select white bread and push start.

"Never let child risk failure, until he has a reasonable chance of success."
— Maria Montessori

Fresh herbs are best for this recipe... triple the measurement of herbs.

FLUFFY ORANGE PANCAKES

1½ cups flour
2 teaspoons baking powder
½ teaspoon salt
3 tablespoons sugar
2 eggs, separated

1 cup milk
½ cup orange juice
3 tablespoons butter, melted
1 tablespoon grated orange peel

Sift flour with baking powder, salt and sugar into bowl. In another bowl, lightly beat egg yolks. Beat in milk, orange juice, butter and orange peel. Add liquid dry ingredients and stir until well blended. Beat egg whites until soft peaks form and fold into batter. Bake on hot, lightly greased griddle. Serve with orange butter and fresh or frozen strawberries or peaches.

ORANGE BUTTER:
½ cup softened butter
1 cup confectioners' sugar

2 tablespoons grated orange peel

Mix the 3 ingredients. Refrigerate unused orange butter for use on toast or waffles.

"Education should no longer be mostly the imparting of knowledge, but must take a new path, seeking the release of human potentialities."

— Maria Montessori

DUTCH APPLE PUFF PANCAKE

2 tablespoons butter
1-2 medium apples, sliced
1 tablespoon sugar
¾ cup flour

½ cup milk
2 eggs beaten
1 teaspoon cinnamon

Preheat oven to 425°. Place butter in pie pan, place in oven just until butter melts. Remove from oven and layer sliced apples evenly on bottom of pan. In a medium mixing bowl, combine the other ingredients. Bake 20-25 minutes, until golden and puffy.

STRAWBERRY FIELDS OVEN PANCAKES

2 pints fresh strawberries	3 tablespoons butter
1/4 cup brown sugar	confectioners' sugar
3 tablespoons flour	1/2 cup sour cream (optional)
1/2 teaspoon salt	1 1/2 tablespoons granulated
1 cup half-and-half	sugar (optional)
8 eggs	

Preheat oven to 450°. Hull strawberries, slice in half, place them in a medium bowl, and toss together with brown sugar. Set aside. In a large bowl, combine flour and salt. Gradually beat in half-and-half. Beat eggs, one at a time into flour mixture, blending until batter is smooth and thin. Place about 1/2 tablespoon butter in each of six 5-6" individual baking dishes (or Pyrex bowls). Place dishes on a baking sheet and preheat in the oven for 4-5 minutes, only long enough to melt the butter. Remove them from the oven and place about 1/2 cup of batter in each dish. Bake for 15 minutes or until cakes are puffed and brown around the edges. Leave cakes in dishes, sprinkle with powdered sugar and pile with strawberries. Each cake may be topped with a spoonful of sour cream, sweetened with the granulated sugar. Serve at once.

FRENCH TOAST CASSEROLE

1 loaf French or Italian bread	3/4 teaspoon salt
8 large eggs	1 tablespoon vanilla
3 cups milk	2 tablespoons butter, cut in
4 teaspoons sugar	small pieces

Grease a 13 x 9" pan. Cut bread into 1" thick pieces and arrange in one layer on bottom of pan. Beat eggs with remaining ingredients, except butter, and pour over bread in pan. Cover with foil and refrigerate 4-36 hours. Bake, uncovered, at 350° for 45-50 minutes, or until puffy and lightly browned. Let stand 5 minutes before serving. Top with hot maple syrup and serve with bacon or sausage.

Starting the first week of April and lasting until the end of May, Hilton Head Islanders journey slightly north of Beaufort to St. Helena Island to a favorite U-Pick-Em Strawberry Patch. Scott Hill Farms guarantees all the delicious fresh berries you can eat — and then some! Remember your way down the country lanes for these same farmers open an unbeatable Pumpkin Patch in October!

PEACH OMELET

3 peaches, peeled and pitted
4 tablespoons butter
3 tablespoons lemon juice
5 eggs

¹/₄ teaspoon dry nutmeg or
    freshly grated nutmeg
salt to taste

Cut the peaches into chunks. In a heavy saucepan melt 2 tablespoons butter. Add the peaches and the lemon juice and cook over high heat, briefly, 1-2 minutes. Remove and keep warm. Beat the eggs with 1 tablespoon of water until frothy. Heat the remaining butter until sizzling in a small frying pan. Pour in the beaten eggs and stir. Let the eggs cook for about 2 minutes, then peel back the set eggs and tip the pan to cook the raw portion. Do this until the eggs are completely cooked, but not overdone. Add the peaches, placing them over one-half of the eggs. Sprinkle with nutmeg and salt to taste. Fold the other half of the eggs over the peaches. Slide omelet out of pan and onto plate.

CREPES

4 eggs, separated
1 pint milk
1 tablespoon sugar

10 heaping tablespoons flour
¹/₂ teaspoon salt
¹/₂ cup butter, melted

Place a metal or copper bowl in freezer for a few minutes, this bowl is for egg whites. Meanwhile, in a medium bowl, beat yolks with salt and sugar, add some milk to mix until mixture is smooth. Add the flour and remaining milk and melted butter to egg yolk mixture, mix well. Put egg whites in frozen bowl and beat until peaks form. Gently fold egg whites into egg and flour mixture.

To prepare crepes, heat pan with a small amount of butter, let the butter melt, pour in enough crepe batter to thinly cover the pan. Just when it's almost done, flip over and heat other side for one minute. Place on plate and spread with your favorite jam or preserves, roll and sprinkle with powdered sugar.

Don't settle for the standard grocery store variety of peach while in South Carolina during the summer. Rustic, roadside stands dot most major highways along the coast and inland. Each one sells extra large, extra juicy South Carolina or Georgia-grown peaches fresh from the trees!

GRITS SOUFFLE

4¹/₂ cups water	4 eggs, slightly beaten
¹/₂ teaspoon salt	¹/₄ teaspoon garlic powder
2 teaspoons sugar	dash Tabasco sauce
1 cup hominy grits (quick cooking)	2 cups grated cheddar cheese
¹/₂ cup butter or margarine cut into pieces	¹/₃ cup bread crumbs
	¹/₂ teaspoon paprika

Preheat oven to 350°. In a heavy 3-4 quart saucepan, bring the water to boiling and add salt, sugar and grits. Cook 3-5 minutes, stirring constantly. Remove the saucepan from heat and add butter, eggs, garlic powder, Tabasco, and cheese. Stir well to blend thoroughly. Pour into a 2¹/₂ quart greased casserole. Sprinkle with bread crumbs and paprika. Bake uncovered for 1 hour. Serve at once.

BAKED GARLIC CHEESE GRITS

4 cups water	¹/₂ cup margarine
2 teaspoons salt	1 roll garlic cheese
1 cup quick cooking grits (not instant)	3 eggs, beaten

Preheat oven to 350°. In a saucepan on the cooktop, bring water to a boil, add salt and grits. Cover and cook over reduced heat until thickened, stirring frequently. Cut up margarine and cheese roll and add to grits. Cover and let melt in cooked grits. Then add beaten eggs and whisk together. Pour into greased casserole dish and bake uncovered for 1 hour.

Perhaps the most famous of Southern foods. Breakfast in the South isn't the same without grits. This nostalgic milled corn cereal has become a popular dinner accompaniment, served as a souffle, baked with garlic or mixed with shrimp and tasso ham. Never underestimate the power of a great dish of grits!

SPINACH & CHEESE FRITTATA

1/2 cup butter or margarine
3 eggs
1 cup flour
1 cup milk
1 teaspoon salt
1 teaspoon baking powder

1 pound Monterey Jack cheese, grated
4 cups fresh spinach, washed, dried, and torn into bite sized pieces

Preheat oven to 350°. Melt butter in a 7 x 11" baking dish. Beat eggs and add remaining ingredients, blending well. Pour spinach mixture over the melted butter. Bake for 40-45 minutes, until golden brown. Cool 10 minutes and serve. This freezes well.

CHEESY BACON & EGG CASSEROLE

1/2 loaf unsliced white bread
5 ounces grated cheddar cheese
5 slices bacon, fried and crumbled
3 shallots, chopped
1 small green bell pepper, chopped
6 eggs, well beaten
2 cups milk

1 teaspoon dry mustard
1 teaspoon Worcestershire sauce
1 tablespoon mayonnaise
black pepper to taste
1/2 teaspoon dried basil leaves
1 small red bell pepper, chopped

Preheat oven to 350°. Trim crust from bread, cut bread into 1" cubes and place in single layer in ovenproof dish. Sprinkle with cheese, bacon, shallots and green pepper. In separate bowl, mix together eggs, milk, mustard, Worcestershire, mayonnaise, pepper and basil. Pour egg mixture over the bread and cheese. Top with red bell pepper. Cover overnight. Bake for one hour or until set. Great for brunch, serve with fresh fruit salad.

OVERNIGHT BREAKFAST SAUSAGE CASSEROLE

1 pound mild bulk sausage	1/2 teaspoon dry mustard
6 slices bread, toasted	salt and pepper to taste
6 eggs	1 cup grated cheddar cheese
2 cups milk	

Preheat oven to 325°. Brown the sausage; drain. Cut each slice of toast into 4 pieces. Beat together the eggs, milk, and seasonings. In a casserole dish, layer half the toast, half the sausage, and half the cheese. Pour half the custard over the layers. Repeat layers once more. Cover and bake for 45 minutes to one hour. Let stand for 5 minutes before serving. Casserole is best made 24 hours ahead and refrigerated until ready to bake.

"Go to your banquet then, but use delight, so as to rise still with an appetite."

CHILES RELLENOS CASSEROLE

8 ounces Mozzarella cheese, grated	1 8-ounce can green chiles
8 ounces cheddar cheese, grated	2 eggs
8 ounces Monterey Jack cheese, grated	2 cups milk
	1/2 cup flour

Preheat oven to 350°. Mix cheeses together. Layer cheese and chiles in a 9 1/2 x 13" casserole dish, beginning and ending with cheese. In separate bowl beat eggs, add milk and flour. Pour over casserole and bake for 45-50 minutes. Good served with enchiladas, guacamole, salad and tortilla chips.

EGGS RO★TEL

8 eggs
1/2 pound fresh mushrooms
3 green onions, chopped
3-4 tablespoons melted
   butter

1 10-ounce can Ro★tel
   tomatoes and green chiles
2 cups grated cheddar cheese
   salt and pepper to taste

In a skillet sauté mushrooms and onions in butter. When soft, add tomatoes and mash all together. Break eggs over mixture, be careful not to break the yolks. Add the salt and pepper, cover with cheese. Simmer until eggs are hard cooked or desired doneness. Spoon onto a plate and enjoy. Great for a holiday brunch.

VIDALIA ONION PIE

9" pie shell
1 cup Swiss cheese, grated
3 cups thinly sliced Vidalia
   onions
3 tablespoons butter
1 cup plain yogurt

1/2 cup heavy cream
2 eggs, beaten
salt and pepper to taste
1/8 teaspoon nutmeg
1/8 teaspoon ginger

Preheat oven to 450°. Prepare pie shell, set aside. Sauté onions in butter until soft and golden. Add all other ingredients to onions and mix well. Turn onion mixture into pie shell and bake in oven at 450° for 10 minutes. Reduce heat to 350° and cook 30 minutes longer or until done. This freezes well.

Vidalia Onions hail from nearby Vidalia, Georgia, and are large, pale yellow onions extremely sweet and juicy. In season from May through June, Vidalias can be purchased at local grocery stores or at roadside produce stands.

SHEPHERD'S QUICHE

3/4 pound lean ground beef	3 eggs
1/4 cup chopped onion	1/4 cup mayonnaise
salt and pepper	2 cups grated cheddar cheese
1/2 cup milk	9" pie shell

Preheat oven to 350°. In skillet, brown ground beef and onion.
Drain well, add salt and pepper. Combine eggs, milk and
mayonnaise, then add cheese. Add ground beef to this mixture
and pour into pie shell. Bake for 35-40 minutes. Let stand
5 minutes before cutting.

CRAB PEPPER QUICHE

8 ounces white crab meat	1/4 cup chopped onion
1/4 cup mayonnaise	1/4 cup chopped bell pepper
1/4 cup milk	9" pie shell
4 ounces grated Swiss cheese	
4 ounces grated cheddar cheese	

Preheat oven to 350°. Brown pie shell lightly, cool. Beat eggs,
stir in milk and flour, add all other ingredients except crab
meat, then gently fold crab meat into the mixture. Pour mixture into pie shell, bake 40 minutes or until done.

JONI'S CUSTARD QUICHE

2 9"-deep dish pie shells	**1 pound cheddar cheese,**
10 strips of cooked bacon or	**grated**
ham	**3/4 cup chopped onion**
10-12 mushrooms, sautéed	
1 1/2 pounds of Swiss cheese,	
grated	

CUSTARD FILLING:

1 tablespoon of flour	**1 teaspoon ground pepper**
4 eggs	**1/4 teaspoon salt**
1 pint half and half	**1/4 teaspoon nutmeg**

Preheat oven to 350°. To prepare custard, blend custard ingredients together with a whisk or a fork. Sprinkle bacon and mushrooms evenly in the bottom of each pie shell. Sprinkle thin layer of some of the cheese on each pie, then add the onion then the remaining cheese. Pour custard filling evenly into both pie shells. Bake for 45-50 minutes.

NO CRUST ZUCCHINI GARDEN QUICHE

2-3 medium zucchini grated	**1 cup Bisquick**
(6 cups)	**1/4 cup vegetable oil**
1 cup grated Swiss cheese	**1/4 teaspoon Italian seasoning**
4 eggs, beaten	

Preheat oven to 400°. Grease a 9" pie plate. In a large bowl, combine all ingredients; mix using a fork. Pour into prepared pie plate. Bake 30-35 minutes, until golden brown. Recipe can be doubled and baked in a 9 x 13" pan.

I have often thought what a melancholy world this would be without children; and what an inhuman world, without the aged.

PICNIC DATE CAKE

1 cup chopped dates
1¼ cups boiling water
¾ teaspoon baking soda
¾ cup shortening
1 cup sugar
2 eggs

1 teaspoon vanilla
1¼ cups plus 2 tablespoons
   flour
1 teaspoon cinnamon
1 teaspoon baking soda
½ teaspoon salt

TOPPING:
½ cup pecans
½ cup brown sugar

½ cup chocolate chips

Preheat oven to 325°. In a medium mixing bowl combine dates, boiling water and baking soda, mix and set aside to cool. In another bowl cream together shortening, sugar, eggs, and vanilla. Add date mixture to creamed mixture.

In another bowl mix together the flour, cinnamon, soda and salt. Add this to the date and creamed mixture. Pour into a greased 8″ x 12″ Pyrex baking dish or similar dish. In a small bowl combine pecans, brown sugar and chocolate chips, sprinkle over top of cake batter. Bake for 40 minutes. Raise oven temperature to 350° if not using Pyrex.

Food for thought: At your next brunch, add a splash of pineapple juice to orange juice. It brings out the orange flavor.

BRITTANY'S APPLE SQUARES

3-4 apples, diced
1 cup flour
1 cup sugar
2 eggs

1 teaspoon baking powder
1/2 teaspoon cinnamon
3/4 cup chopped nuts

Preheat oven to 350°. In a bowl, combine sugar, eggs and apples, then add the other ingredients, mix gently but thoroughly. Pour mixture into 8 x 8″ greased pan and bake for 45 minutes. Serve warm with whipped cream, also is a great lunch box snack.

OUR FAVORITE
SOUR CREAM COFFEECAKE

1/2 cup butter, softened
1 cup sugar
2 eggs
1 teaspoon vanilla
1 cup cake flour

1/2 cup all-purpose flour
1 1/2 teaspoons baking powder
1 teaspoon baking soda
1/4 teaspoon salt
1 cup sour cream

TOPPING:
1 1/2 teaspoons ground
   cinnamon
4 tablespoons sugar

1/2 cup raisins
1/2 cup chopped walnuts

Everyone has their favorite sour cream coffee cake recipe. This one is ours!

Grease and flour an 8 or 9" springform pan. In a large bowl, cream together the butter and 1 cup sugar until light and fluffy. Blend in the eggs, one at a time, beating after each addition, and the vanilla. In another bowl, sift together the flours, baking powder, baking soda, and salt. Slowly blend the flour mixture into the creamed mixture until smooth. Blend the sour cream into the batter, mixing well. Pour 1/2 the mixture into the prepared pan.

In another bowl mix together the cinnamon, sugar, and raisins and sprinkle 1/2 of this mixture evenly over the batter in the pan. Top with remaining batter, remaining cinnamon mixture, and the walnuts. Bake in a preheated 350° oven for 40-45 minutes or until a toothpick inserted in the center comes out clean. Cool in the pan on a rack for about 20 minutes. Serve warm, cut in wedges. For chocolate lovers, add mini-chocolate chips to the topping.

Soups & Salads

SALADS & SOUPS

MARINATED ASPARAGUS SALAD

1 can asparagus (drained) or
  $\frac{1}{2}$ pound fresh asparagus,
  steamed
$\frac{1}{2}$ cup sugar
$\frac{1}{4}$ cup white vinegar

$\frac{1}{4}$ cup water
3 whole cloves
1 cinnamon stick
$\frac{1}{2}$ teaspoon celery seed
$\frac{1}{2}$ teaspoon salt

Place drained asparagus in glass casserole or Tupperware container. In small saucepan, heat sugar, vinegar and water to boiling. Add cloves, cinnamon, celery seed and salt. Stir and pour over asparagus. Cool and refrigerate at least 4 hours or overnight. Recipe doubles easily.

BELL PEPPER SALAD WITH FETA CHEESE

3 tablespoons red wine
  vinegar
1 tablespoon water
$1\frac{1}{2}$ teaspoons olive oil
$\frac{1}{2}$ teaspoon Dijon mustard
$\frac{3}{4}$ teaspoon dried whole
  oregano
$\frac{1}{8}$ teaspoon salt
1 clove garlic, minced
$\frac{3}{4}$ cup thinly sliced purple
  onion

6 plum tomatoes, cut
  lengthwise into $\frac{1}{8}$" slices
2 medium size yellow
  peppers, cut into $\frac{1}{8}$" rings
$\frac{1}{4}$ cup crumbled Feta cheese
  (1 ounce)
fresh ground pepper
fresh oregano sprigs (optional)

Combine first seven ingredients in a jar for vinaigrette. Cover tightly and shake vigorously. In a small bowl, combine 1 tablespoon of vinaigrette and onions, stir well. Spoon onion mixture evenly onto a serving platter. Arrange tomato around edge of platter. Place peppers in center of platter on top of onion. Drizzle remaining vinaigrette mixture over peppers and onions. Top with crumbled Feta and pepper to taste. Garnish with oregano.

WATERCRESS WITH RASPBERRIES

4 cups fresh watercress, tough stems removed
1 red onion, thinly sliced

1 cup walnuts, coarsely chopped and toasted

DRESSING:
1¼ cups fresh raspberries
¼ cup walnut or olive oil
1 orange rind, grated
½ cup fresh orange juice

3 tablespoons raspberry vinegar
1 teaspoon honey
fresh pepper

Clean watercress and set aside. Set aside thinly sliced red onion. Spread walnuts on cookie sheet and bake in 350° oven 5 minutes until toasted. Next, mix the dressing, force ¼ cup raspberries through a sieve and into a jar. Add the remaining ingredients and shake well. Toss together watercress, onion, walnuts and 1 cup of raspberries with dressing. Serve.

Food for thought: Watercress is a good source of vitamin C, iron and beta carotene

ORANGE WATERCRESS SALAD

1 head Belgian endive, coarsely chopped
3 bunches watercress, washed, tough stems removed

2 oranges, peeled, seeded and sectioned (cut sections in half)

DRESSING:
1 orange rind, grated
⅓ cup olive oil
3 tablespoons white wine vinegar

1 teaspoon Dijon mustard
1 teaspoon chopped parsley
1 tablespoon grated Parmesan cheese

Put the greens in your serving bowl with orange pieces; refrigerate until ready to serve. In a jar add all other ingredients and shake well to mix. A whisk in a bowl will work also. Refrigerate. When ready, pour dressing over salad and toss gently.

CALIFORNIA CITRUS SPINACH SALAD

1 or 2 bunches of spinach, cleaned and stemmed
1 or 2 grapefruits, sectioned and peeled

1 avocado, sliced and diced
5-7 slices of crispy bacon
1/2 pound Gruyère cheese, grated

DRESSING:
1/2 cup sugar
1 teaspoon dry mustard
5 1/2 tablespoons red wine vinegar
1 teaspoon salt

1/2 teaspoon pepper
1 1/2 teaspoons grated onion
2 1/2 teaspoons poppy seeds
1 cup oil

Combine ingredients for dressing and chill overnight. Gently toss the salad ingredients together with dressing, add dressing to taste. Don't over toss or grapefruit will disintegrate.

TRADITIONAL SPINACH SALAD

1 bag fresh spinach
1 can bean sprouts, drained
1 can water chestnuts, drained and chopped
3 hard boiled eggs, chopped

1 pound bacon, fried and crumbled
1 or 2 bunches of spring onions sliced tops and all

DRESSING:
1 cup salad oil
1/3 cup catsup
1 tablespoon Worcestershire sauce

1/2 cup sugar
1/4 cup vinegar

Mix all dressing ingredients together in a blender. In salad bowl gently toss salad ingredients; add dressing to taste.

THE ULTIMATE SALAD

1 14-ounce can artichoke hearts, drained and quartered
1 cup fresh English peas, cooked or 1 10-ounce package frozen peas, thawed and drained
1 large red onion, thinly sliced

lettuce mixture; iceberg, bibb, romaine, and red leaf lettuce
1/2 cup bleu cheese, crumbled
2 ripe avocados, sliced and tossed in lemon juice
1 can mandarin oranges drained

DRESSING:
3/4 cup oil
1/4 cup wine vinegar
1/2 teaspoon salt

1/2 teaspoon sugar
1/4 teaspoon pepper

Combine ingredients for dressing. Combine artichoke hearts, peas and onions, marinate overnight in dressing. To prepare salad tear washed, chilled greens and place in a glass serving bowl lined with red leaf lettuce. Add bleu cheese, avocado, marinated vegetables and mandarin oranges. Toss well and serve. Variation: chicken or shrimp may be added for main course.

ANTIPASTO

Italian salami
pepperoni
sharp provolone cheese
Mozzarella cheese
black olives

green olives
marinated artichokes
marinated mushrooms
pepperoncini
pimentos

Drain all cans or jars, discard juices. Combine all ingredients, except meats and cheeses, in a bowl for several hours before serving. Refrigerate. Just before serving add chunks of cheese and thin slices of meat and mix well. Serve in small bowls with Italian bread or breadsticks. Vary the ingredients and the amounts according to personal taste and the size of the crowd.

BROCCOLI, RAISIN & PINE NUT SALAD

6 cups uncooked broccoli florets

2 cups shredded red cabbage

2 tablespoons plus 2 teaspoons pine nuts

2 tablespoons reduced fat mayonnaise

2 tablespoons non-fat sour cream

1 tablespoon plus 1 teaspoon firmly packed dark brown sugar

1 tablespoon white vinegar

2 tablespoons raisins

1 1/2 scallions, finely chopped

3 slices crisp bacon, crumbled

Preheat oven to 300°. Toast pine nuts 3 minutes, let cool. Meanwhile, in a small bowl with a fork combine mayonnaise, sour cream, brown sugar and vinegar, blend until smooth, set aside. In medium bowl add broccoli, raisins, scallions, pine nuts and bacon. Drizzle in dressing. Toss to coat well, cover, refrigerate 24 hours. To serve: place 1/2 cup shredded cabbage on dish, top with 1 1/2 cups marinated broccoli salad.

CHILLED BROCCOLI STICKS

1 bunch of broccoli, stems only

1 large tomato, peeled, seeded and chopped

1 clove garlic, minced

1/4 teaspoon salt

2 teaspoons lemon juice

1 teaspoon red wine vinegar

1/4 cup olive oil or vegetable oil

3 tablespoons grated Parmesan cheese

pepper to taste

Trim broccoli stems well with a vegetable peeler and cut in 2" lengths, then slice these into matchsticks. Place in a bowl and toss with tomato. In a small bowl, mix the minced garlic and salt together. Whisk in lemon juice, wine vinegar, and olive oil. Pour over broccoli sticks and toss well, then toss with Parmesan cheese and pepper. Cover and chill 1 hour or more before serving.

PATTE'S PARSLEY & CARROT SALAD

3 cups grated carrots
1 bunch fresh parsley, rinsed
    and finely chopped (about
    2 cups)
1 clove roasted garlic

3 tablespoons fresh lemon
    juice
1/4 cup canola oil
1/2 teaspoon salt
fresh ground pepper to taste

Combine carrots, parsley, garlic, lemon juice, oil, salt and pepper in a serving bowl and toss well. Can be made ahead of time and refrigerated. Will keep for 2 or 3 days.

*Food for thought:
Parsley,
a natural breath
deodorizer...
Parsley is an
excellent source
of vitamins A & C.
For some it has an
addictive quality.
Our cover artist
has been caught
eating the parsley
garnish at parties.*

MARINATED CARROT SALAD

2 1/2 pounds carrots, peeled
    and sliced

1 small purple onion, sliced
    and rings separated

DRESSING:
1 cup white vinegar
1 cup water
2 tablespoons olive oil
3/4 cup sugar

2 cloves garlic crushed
1 1/2 teaspoons seasoned salt
1/2 teaspoon dry mustard

Combine carrots and onions in bowl; set aside. In another bowl, combine dressing ingredients, stir until sugar dissolves. Pour over carrots and onions toss gently. Cover and chill at least 8 hours. Before serving, drain dressing. Spoon carrots and onions onto a platter lined with leaf lettuce. Decorate platter with radishes and yellow pepper slices if desired.

TOMATO & FETA SALAD

2 pints cherry tomatoes
2 cloves of garlic, peeled
1/2 cup pitted ripe olives

1 1/2 cups crumbled Feta
  cheese

DRESSING:
1/3 cup olive oil
1/2 cup plus 2 teaspoons wine
  vinegar
1 teaspoon dried whole
  oregano

1 teaspoon dried whole
  thyme
salt and pepper to taste

Rinse cherry tomatoes and cut in half, set aside. Rub inside of salad bowl with garlic; discard garlic. Combine tomatoes, olives, and cheese in salad bowl. Combine remaining ingredients in a jar. Cover tightly and shake vigorously. Pour over tomato mixture, tossing gently. Refrigerate at least four hours before serving.

TOMATO MELÁNGE

6 ripe tomatoes

DRESSING:
2/3 cup oil
1/4 cup wine vinegar
1/4 cup chopped parsley
1/4 cup grated onions
1 teaspoon salt

1/4 teaspoon ground pepper
2 teaspoons marjoram or
  thyme
1 clove garlic, minced

Peel and slice tomatoes. Place in deep bowl. In jar or cruet, combine oil, vinegar, and seasonings. Shake well. Pour over tomatoes. Cover and chill at least several hours or overnight, occasionally spooning the dressing over tomatoes. At serving time, spoon dressing over again. Transfer tomatoes to serving platter.

Food for thought:
The average
person
consumes
17 pounds of
tomatoes
per year.

SUPER COLE SLAW

Have you ever tried jazzing up your cole slaw with a few dashes of Tabasco?

1 large cabbage, shredded
2 red onions, chopped

1 bell pepper (green, yellow, red, or purple), chopped
1 cucumber, chopped

DRESSING:
1 cup red wine vinegar
3/4 cup oil
1 teaspoon celery seed

1 teaspoon dry mustard
1 tablespoon salt

Mix together cabbage, onions and peppers. Combine dressing ingredients in saucepan. Bring to rolling boil, pour over cabbage mixture. Cover and chill at least 4 hours, the longer the better. Chop cucumber and toss in just before serving. Serves 20.

TABBOULEH SALAD

1 cup bulgar wheat
3 tomatoes, peeled and chopped
1 cucumber, peeled, seeded and chopped
1/2 cup thinly sliced radishes
1/2 cup chopped green onions with parts of tops

1/2 cup fresh parsley, minced
2 tablespoons fresh mint, minced
juice of 1 lemon
1/2 cup olive oil
salt and pepper to taste

Pour boiling water over the bulgar wheat, just enough to cover. Cover bowl and let sit 1 hour. Water should be completely absorbed, if not drain off excess water. Mix in vegetables and herbs, then toss with lemon juice, olive oil, and salt and pepper to taste. Can be served immediately or chilled several hours before serving.

FROSTY ORANGE SALAD

1 small package orange Jello
1 cup boiling water
1/2 pint orange sherbet

1 cup Cool Whip
2 cans mandarin oranges, drained

Dissolve Jello in boiling water; immediately add orange sherbet and stir until melted. Chill until thickened (approximately 1 hour). Whip until foamy, fold in Cool Whip and 1 1/2 cans of mandarin oranges. Arrange remaining oranges on bottom of a Jello mold. Place gelatin on top of mandarin oranges and put in refrigerator. Unmold and serve. Best if made the day before serving.

CRANBERRY SALAD

1 large cherry or strawberry Jello
2 cups uncooked fresh cranberries
1 orange (cut orange in sections, leave rind on)

1 large red apple chopped
1 cup celery diced
1 cup sugar
1 cup chopped walnuts

Mix Jello with 1 1/2 cups boiling water; stir until dissolved and let cool. Grind cranberries and oranges in blender or food processor putting small amounts in blender to ease grinding. Put cranberries and oranges in a bowl, add celery, apple and nuts. Stir in sugar. Put in Jello mold or pie plate. Pour Jello over cranberry mixture. Refrigerate until set. Great with chicken or turkey.

Food for thought: To freshen limp celery, cut a washed and peeled potato into several pieces. Place the potato and celery into a container; cover with water and refrigerate for a few hours for crisper stalks!

ROSE RICE SALAD

1 package Uncle Ben's wild
  rice
1 6-ounce jar marinated
  artichokes

1 small red onion
2 cups cooked chicken or
  ham

DRESSING:
1/4 cup salad oil
1 tablespoon lemon juice
1 tablespoon wine vinegar
1 teaspoon sugar

1/4 teaspoon salt
1/4 teaspoon dry mustard
1/4 cup paprika
dash red pepper

Cook rice as directed. Mix all ingredients together. Combine dressing ingredients and toss with rice salad. Can be served room temperature or cold.

WARM SCALLOP SALAD WITH TOMATO, MINT & LIME

1 pound scallops
2 tablespoons olive oil
1/4 teaspoon salt

pinch cracked black pepper
2 bunches fresh spinach

DRESSING:
1/3 cup olive oil
2 medium shallots, finely
  chopped
2 tablespoons lime juice
1/2 teaspoon salt

1/2 teaspoon coarsely cracked
  black pepper
2 medium tomatoes, peeled,
  seeded and chopped
2 tablespoons fresh mint,
  finely chopped

For dressing: Heat olive oil in medium skillet. Add shallots and sauté 2 minutes or until soft. Add lime juice, salt and pepper. Remove from heat and add tomatoes and mint. Set aside.

Drain scallops and pat dry. If scallops are 1" in diameter or larger, cut in half before using. In another medium skillet heat 2 tablespoons olive oil. Add scallops and sauté over medium-high heat for 3-5 minutes, turning often. They should be slightly translucent in the middle. Remove from heat. Pour half of dressing mixture over warm scallops, add salt and pepper and mix. Divide spinach evenly among individual plates. Spoon scallops with some dressing in center of each plate. Spoon additional tomato mint dressing around scallops.

SEAFOOD PASTA SALAD WITH LEMON-DILL DRESSING

2 tablespoons olive oil
1 teaspoon salt
1 pound small pasta shells
1/4 pound Chinese snow peas
1 cup water
1 cup dry white wine
1 bay leaf
1 pound raw medium shrimp, shelled and deveined

1 small red bell pepper, seeded and julienned
1 small onion, chopped
1/2 cup Greek olives, pitted
1 medium carrot, peeled and julienned
1/2 pound cooked crabmeat, torn into small pieces

DRESSING:
3 tablespoons finely chopped fresh dill
2 medium cloves garlic minced
1/2 cup lemon juice

1/2 cup olive oil
1 teaspoon salt
1/4 teaspoon finely ground pepper

Add 1 tablespoon olive oil and salt to large pot of boiling water. Add pasta shells and cook over high heat 10 minutes or until al dente. Drain and remove to bowl of ice water mixed with 1 tablespoon olive oil until cool. Drain thoroughly. Immerse snow peas in a small saucepan of boiling water and boil 1 minute. Drain and pour cold water over to stop cooking process. Drain thoroughly. Place in large bowl.

Combine water, wine and bay leaf in medium saucepan and bring to boil. Add shrimp and cook over low heat for 3-5 minutes or until shrimp are pink on outside and just cooked in center. Remove with slotted spoon to bowl. Immerse red pepper in shrimp-cooking liquid and boil 1 minute. Drain and pour cold water over pepper to stop cooking process. Drain thoroughly. Put in large mixing bowl. Add onions, olives, carrot, and crabmeat.

In a small bowl combine dill, garlic and lemon juice. Whisk in olive oil slowly until blended. Season with salt and pepper. Add drained pasta to large mixing bowl of ingredients. Add dressing and toss to coat ingredients. Taste for seasoning. Chill or serve at room temperature. May be refrigerated up to 4 hours. Remove from refrigerator 1/2 hour before serving.

"The child is mysterious and powerful and contains within the secret of human nature."
— Maria Montessori

CHICKEN, BROCCOLI & PASTA WITH BASIL MAYONNAISE DRESSING

2 whole chicken breasts	3 cups small fresh broccoli
1 tablespoon butter or	florets
margarine, melted	2 medium size tomatoes,
8 ounces rotelle or penne	cut in wedges
pasta	

DRESSING:

1/2 cup toasted walnut pieces	1/2 cup freshly grated
1 cup mayonnaise	Parmesan cheese
1/2 cup packed fresh basil	1 tablespoon lemon juice
leaves	2 teaspoons coarsely
	chopped garlic

Food for thought: To extract lemon juice more easily, warm the lemons in a bowl of hot tap water before cutting, and squeezing juice.

For dressing: Toast walnuts in single layer on baking sheet in preheated 350° oven 5-7 minutes. Cool. Put walnut pieces in blender or food processor. Add mayonnaise, basil, Parmesan cheese, lemon juice and garlic. Process until smooth.

Preheat oven to 375°. Arrange chicken breasts in a single layer in a roasting pan; brush with butter. Bake for 20-25 minutes until chicken is springy to touch and just cooked through. Chill until cool enough to handle then tear into narrow strips, discarding skin and bones. Cook pasta according to package directions, adding broccoli to pot during the last 2 minutes of cooking time. Drain; place under cold water to cool and to prevent pasta from sticking; drain again; put in large bowl. Toss chicken strips, broccoli, pasta and tomatoes with enough dressing to moisten. Mound salad on a platter. Serve remaining dressing on the side.

Try green beans or zucchini instead of broccoli or use a mixture of all three.

GREEK PASTA SALAD

1 pound tri-color Rotini pasta, cooked and drained
1 green bell pepper, chopped
1 red bell pepper, chopped
1 cucumber, seeded, peeled and chopped

1 can kidney beans, drained
1 can chick peas, drained
8 ounces Feta cheese in chunks/crumbled

DRESSING:
1 part Balsamic vinegar
1 part lemon juice

1 part extra virgin olive oil
salt, pepper & oregano to taste

In jar or cruet mix the dressing, set aside. Mix all the salad ingredients and toss with dressing. Allow to marinate in refrigerator overnight. Serve with garlic bread; or for dinner with grilled tuna or chicken or Italian sausage.

MARINATED GOLDEN & RED PEPPERS

3 red bell peppers

3 yellow bell peppers

DRESSING:
2 teaspoons lemon juice
3 tablespoons red wine vinegar
1 medium clove garlic, minced

1 teaspoon anchovy paste
1/8 teaspoon salt
pinch finely ground pepper
6 tablespoons olive oil

GARNISH:
2 tablespoons finely chopped basil

2 tablespoons small black nicoise olives

For dressing: Combine all ingredients except oil and mix well. Whisk in oil slowly. Set aside.

To peel peppers, place on broiler pan and broil approximately 6" from heat until blackened on all sides. Use tongs to turn peppers. Put peppers in plastic bag and close tightly. Let rest for 10 minutes. Remove peppers from bag. Drain peppers and peel off skin. Make a slit in each pepper and open it up. Core and cut off stem. Scrape off seeds and ribs from peppers. With a sharp knife or pizza wheel, cut peppers in 1/2" wide strips. Place in serving dish and pour dressing over. Sprinkle with chopped basil and decorate with small olives. Serve at room temperature or slightly chilled. May be kept up to 5 days in refrigerator. Remove from refrigerator 2 hours prior to serving so that dressing is clear and just slightly chilled. Add garnish just before serving.

Food for thought: Balsamic vinegar is made from white Trebiano grape juice which gets its dark color from aging in wood barrels over a period of years.

SAN VICENTE CHICKEN SALAD

4 boneless, skinless chicken
  breasts
$1/2$ to 1 cup mayonnaise
1 cup raisins

1 cup chopped celery
$1/2$ cup pecans (optional)
fresh dill or dried dill to taste
salt and pepper to taste

Boil chicken breasts until done, approximately 20 minutes. Let chicken breasts cool and cut into pieces. Add all other ingredients, taste as you go along; add more or less of ingredients to your liking. Refrigerate at least one hour before serving.

MRS. B'S CHICKEN SALAD

"An adult works to perfect the environment... A child works to perfect himself."
— Maria Montessori

1 whole chicken
1 large bay leaf
1 teaspoon garlic salt
3 or 4 stalks celery, chopped
4 hard boiled eggs, chopped
1 bunch green grapes, halved

mayonnaise to taste
3 tablespoons Durkees
  Famous Sauce
parsley flakes
salt and pepper

Season chicken with pepper and garlic salt. Place in large pot of water with bay leaf. Bring to a boil, cover and simmer for 1 to $1^{1}/_{2}$ hours, until chicken is falling off the bone. Let chicken cool; debone and chop. Mix with celery, eggs and grapes. Add Durkees sauce and mayonnaise until moist. Add salt, pepper and parsley flakes to taste.

ORIENTAL CHICKEN SALAD

Pre-roasted chicken from
   your favorite grocery store
   or homemade roasted
   chicken leftovers
1 head of lettuce, shredded

5 green onions, sliced thin
1/2 cup slivered almonds
1/2 cup sesame seeds toasted*
fresh cilantro, chopped

DRESSING:
1/2 cup peanut oil
2 tablespoons soy sauce
2 tablespoons fresh lemon

1 teaspoon dry mustard
2 teaspoons sugar

In jar or cruet mix dressing ingredients, shake well. *Toast
sesame seeds on cookie sheet in oven at 320° for 5 minutes.
Cut up chicken, then mix all salad ingredients and pour
dressing over all. Toss gently.

REFRESHING CHICKEN FRUIT SALAD

4 chicken breasts
1 large red apple
1 large green apple
1 medium orange, peeled

2 cups seedless grapes
  (red or green)
1 cup raisins
1/2 cup crushed walnuts
1 cup Miracle Whip

Cook chicken, grilled or baked, fried or boiled. Dice into large
pieces. Cut apples, orange and grapes into large diced pieces.
Add raisins and crushed walnuts. Stir in Miracle Whip.
Refreshing and easy to prepare!

TURKEY SALAD MADRAS

2 cups cooked turkey, cubed
1 cup celery, sliced
1 cup seedless grapes, halved

1 cup canned pineapple
  cubes
1/2 cup sliced almonds

DRESSING:
2 tablespoons soy sauce
2 tablespoons lemon juice
1-2 teaspoons curry powder

1/2 cup mayonnaise
1/2 cup sour cream

In small bowl mix ingredients for dressing. Toss with turkey,
celery, grapes, pineapple and almonds. Serve on greens or use
as a filling for pita bread.

*Fresh lemon juice
and stocks may
be conveniently
frozen in ice cube
trays. Store the
frozen cubes in
plastic bags in the
freezer to be used
as needed.*

LOWCOUNTRY SEAFOOD GUMBO

$^1/_4$ pound shrimp
$^1/_4$ pound bay scallops
1 cup olive oil
$^1/_4$ pound swordfish
$^1/_4$ pound mahi-mahi
$^1/_4$ pound grouper
2 medium green bell
  peppers, chopped
$^1/_4$ cup chopped garlic
1 large white onion, chopped

1 small stalk celery, chopped
$^1/_2$ cup dijon mustard
1 16-ounce package frozen
  sliced green okra
4 16-ounce cans diced
  tomatoes in juice
3 chicken bouillon cubes
salt and white pepper to taste
$^3/_4$ of an ounce of
  cajun seasonings

*Captain's Seafood,
a long-time
Lowcountry
restaurant
supplier,
made the leap
three years ago
and opened their
own seafood
restaurant.
Despite the
"no vacancy"
status in our
restaurant section,
their seafood
gumbo was too
tasty to pass up!*

Using an 8 quart soup pot sauté all vegetables together in olive oil, add salt and pepper. Cube the swordfish, mahi-mahi, and grouper into 1 inch pieces. Peel and devein shrimp, remove tails and chop into small pieces. Add fish pieces, shrimp and scallops into the vegetable mixture. Allow to sauté on a medium to medium high heat until fish is done and vegetables are soft. Meanwhile, in a separate mixing bowl add the chicken bouillon cubes to 3 cups hot tap water and dissolve cubes, then add mustard and cajun seasonings. To the soup pot, add tomatoes and okra, then add bouillon mustard mixture. Allow to simmer at medium heat for 30 minutes. Serve with hot corn muffins and honey butter. Note: Add more water for a thinner soup, add more cajun seasoning to spice it up.

CAROLINA CORN, RED PEPPER, & LEEK SOUP

5 ears of corn
2 tablespoons unsalted butter
3 tablespoons oil
3 medium leeks, cleaned and coarsely chopped
1 large red bell pepper, seeded and coarsely chopped
1 1/2 quarts chicken stock
1/2 cup whipping cream
1/2 teaspoon salt
1/8 teaspoon coarsely cracked white pepper
pinch cayenne pepper
2 tablespoons chopped parsley to garnish

Scrape kernels off corncobs using a sharp knife. Reserve 1/4 cup for garnish. In a large saucepan heat butter and oil. Add leeks and sauté over medium heat, stirring occasionally, until soft, about 5 minutes. Add red pepper and continue sautéing for 5 more minutes. They should be slightly soft. Add corn and cook 3 minutes. Add chicken stock and bring to a boil. Reduce heat and simmer slowly, uncovered for 30 minutes. Pour soup into blender or food processor fitted with steel blade and process for one minute. For a smoother textured soup, strain through a food mill and then return to saucepan. Add cream, salt, pepper and cayenne. Reheat over low heat. Taste for seasoning. Pour soup into bowls; garnish with corn and fresh parsley. Note: The raw corn kernels add a nice crunch, you may boil them for 2 minutes and drain if desired.

"Each child carries unseen within him the adult he will become."
— Maria Montessori

POTATO, FENNEL & LEEK SOUP

2 fennel bulbs with 2 inches stalk (approximately 1 pound)
2 medium baking potatoes
3 tablespoons unsalted butter
1 tablespoon vegetable oil
2 medium leeks, white part only, cleaned and coarsely chopped
2 quarts chicken stock
1 teaspoon salt
1/2 teaspoon ground pepper

Remove core from fennel and slice. Reserve some sprigs for garnish. Peel potatoes and chop coarsely. In medium soup pot, heat butter and oil over low heat. Add leeks and sauté, stirring occasionally, until soft. Add fennel and potatoes and continue sautéing for 10 more minutes or until softened. Add chicken stock and bring to simmer. Partially cover and cook 30 minutes. Puree soup in a food processor with steel blade, or in a blender and return to pot. Add salt and pepper, season to taste. Pour into soup bowls and garnish with fennel sprigs.

GAZPACHO

1 medium Vidalia onion	16 ounce can tomatoes
2 cloves garlic	5 tablespoons red wine
1 green bell pepper	vinegar
1 medium cucumber, peeled	$1/3$ cup breadcrumbs
7 cups tomato juice	salt and pepper to taste

In a blender or food processor, puree the onion, garlic, pepper and cucumber. Add the tomato juice, tomatoes, vinegar and breadcrumbs and blend again. Season to taste with salt and pepper. Serve hot or chilled. Garnish with all, some or combination of the following: chopped onion, chopped green pepper, chopped cucumber, grated Parmesan cheese, chopped fresh parsley.

CREAM OF CARROT SOUP

6 large sweet carrots	$1/2$ teaspoon salt
1 medium onion, sliced	pepper to taste
3 cups chicken stock	1 cup whipping cream
1 or 2 bay leaves	3 tablespoons butter
$1/4$ teaspoon sugar	2 tablespoons flour

Clean and chop carrots and onion. In a Dutch oven or similar pot, simmer carrots and onions for 45 minutes in chicken stock with bay leaves, sugar, salt and pepper. Remove bay leaves. Puree until smooth. In Dutch oven, heat butter gradually; stir in the flour until smooth. Add puree and boil 3 minutes, stirring frequently. Remove from heat and add cream. Return to burner to gently heat through.

FRENCH ONION SOUP

3 or 4 medium onions, thinly
  sliced and separated
1/4 cup butter
1 tablespoon flour
1 can chicken broth
1 can beef broth
1/3 cup white wine
3 cups water

1/2 teaspoon fresh ground
  pepper
6 thick slices French bread
  toasted
6 slices mozzarella cheese
1/2 cup fresh grated Parmesan
  cheese

Sauté onion rings in butter until tender. Add flour and stir to
coat evenly. Slowly add chicken broth, beef broth, wine, water
and pepper. Bring to a boil, reduce heat, cover and simmer 30
minutes. Toast French bread slices and place in individual
ovenproof bowls. Ladle soup over toast and top each serving
with slice of mozzarella and fresh Parmesan. Broil 2-4 minutes
until cheese melts and begins to turn golden brown. Serve
immediately.

CHEDDAR BROCCOLI NOODLE SOUP

2 tablespoons oil or
  margarine
3/4 cup chopped onions
6 chicken bouillon cubes
6 cups water
6 ounces fine egg noodles
  (approximately 4 cups)
1 teaspoons salt

2 bunches fresh broccoli or 2
  packages frozen chopped
  broccoli
1/8 teaspoon garlic powder
6 cups milk
1 pound grated cheddar
  cheese
pepper to taste

Sauté onions in oil over medium heat in large saucepan for 5
minutes. Add water and bouillon. Heat to boiling, stirring
occasionally. Gradually add noodles and salt. Cook uncovered for 5 minutes, stirring occasionally. Stir in broccoli and
garlic powder. Cook 4 minutes more. Add milk, cheese, pepper. Stir constantly until cheese melts.

CRAB STEW

6 tablespoons butter
1 large onion, chopped
1 bunch green onions,
  chopped
2 stalks celery, chopped
1 cup water

3 potatoes, peeled and diced
  (1½ cups)
2½ cups lump crabmeat,
  cleaned and picked through
2 cups milk
salt and pepper to taste
Tabasco

Melt the butter in a large pan, add the onion, green onions, and celery. Cook until soft. Add the water and bring to a boil. Add potatoes, and continue to cook until the potatoes are soft. Add crabmeat and milk and heat through without boiling. Season to taste with salt, pepper and a dash of Tabasco. Serve immediately.

THEO'S OYSTER STEW

1-2 pints oysters
1 quart whole milk
¼ cup margarine

oyster crackers
salt and pepper

In a saucepan heat and stir milk and margarine; don't allow to boil. Using a cooking/candy thermometer, when the temperature reaches 170°, add the oysters and stir until oysters curl. Salt and pepper to taste. Pour in warmed bowls and top with oyster crackers.

HARBOURTOWN SCALLOP SOUP WITH CHARDONNAY & SAFFRON

3 tablespoons unsalted butter
3 medium leeks, cleaned and
  finely chopped
1 red bell pepper, seeded and
  thinly julienned
1 quart fish stock
1 cup Chardonnay or other
  dry white wine
1 cup whipping cream
$1/_2$ teaspoon salt

$1/_4$ teaspoon ground pepper
1 generous pinch of saffron
  threads
$1/_4$ pound mushrooms, sliced
$3/_4$ pound swordfish steaks,
  cut into bite size pieces
$3/_4$ pound scallops
2 tablespoons parsley for
  garnish

In medium skillet, heat 2 tablespoons butter over low heat.
Add leeks and sauté, stirring occasionally, for 5 minutes or
until soft. Add red bell pepper and sauté another 2 minutes.
Set aside. In a 4 quart non-aluminum saucepan, combine fish
stock and wine and boil about 10 minutes or until reduced to
about 1 quart. Add cream and boil again for 10 minutes.
Add salt, pepper and saffron. Add leeks and red bell pepper.
In medium skillet, heat 1 tablespoon butter over medium heat.
Add mushrooms and sauté briefly, stirring until cooked but not
browned. Reserve. Heat soup base and add swordfish. Simmer
3 minutes and add scallops. Simmer another 3 minutes or
until just tender and moist but not overdone. Add mushrooms.
Ladle into soup bowls and garnish with parsley.

SPLIT PEA SOUP

1 pound green split peas,
  rinsed
2 quarts water
2 cups carrots, sliced
2 cups celery and tops, sliced
  small

2 cups onion, chopped
$1/_2$ cup parsley, chopped
2 meaty ham bones
1 tablespoon oregano
1 tablespoon salt
$1/_2$ teaspoon black pepper

Cook everything in heavy pot 1 to $1^1/_2$ hours, until thick.
Remove meat from ham bones and return to soup. Discard
bones. Add a little cream if desired.

WINTER THYME LENTIL SOUP

2 tablespoons olive or vegetable oil

2 large or 3 medium onions, chopped

3 carrots, coarsely chopped

$3/4$ teaspoon marjoram, crumbled

$3/4$ teaspoon thyme leaves crumbled

1 28-ounce can coarsely chopped tomatoes with their juice

7 cups broth, beef, or chicken

$1^1/2$ cups dried lentils and picked over

$1/2$ teaspoon salt

$1/4$-$1/2$ teaspoon freshly ground pepper

6 ounces dry white wine

$1/3$ cup chopped fresh parsley or 2 tablespoons dried parsley flakes

$1/2$ cup grated cheddar cheese

Heat the oil in a large saucepan, and sauté the onions, carrots, marjoram and thyme, stirring for about 5 minutes. Add the tomatoes broth and lentils. Bring the soup to a boil, reduce the heat, cover the pan and simmer the soup for about one hour or until the lentils are tender. Add the salt, pepper, wine and parsley and simmer the soup for a few minutes. Serve with cheese sprinkled on each portion.

SENATE BEAN SOUP

2 pounds small navy beans

2 quarts water

$1^1/2$ pounds meaty smoked ham hocks

1 chopped onion

1-2 tablespoons butter

salt and pepper

Rinse beans in several washings of water. In large covered Dutch oven, cook beans and ham hock in water for about 3 hours, until beans are very tender. Add more water if needed. Remove meat from hocks. Discard bones and return meat to soup. Sauté onion in butter and add to soup. Taste. Salt if needed. Pepper heavily.

BLACK BEAN SOUP WITH CUMIN

1 cup dry black beans, soaked
7 cups broth (beef, chicken, or vegetable)
1 tablespoon vegetable oil
1 large onion, minced
1 large clove garlic, minced
1/4 cup diced celery
1/2 cup finely diced carrots

3/4 teaspoon crushed cumin seed, to taste
1/4 teaspoon freshly ground black pepper
1/4 teaspoon salt
1 chopped hard-boiled egg and chopped scallions for garnish

To soak beans, place washed beans in a bowl, cover with cold water, and soak overnight. Or place washed beans in a saucepan, add 4 cups water, bring the beans to a boil, boil for 2 minutes, turn off heat, and let the beans stand for 1 hour. Drain soaked beans. Add broth, bring to a boil, reduce heat to low, and simmer beans, partially covering pan for 2-3 hours or until beans are thoroughly cooked. In a heavy skillet, heat oil, add onion and garlic. Cook, stirring over low heat until transparent. Add celery and carrots and cook mixture, stirring for a few minutes longer. Add vegetables to beans. Season with cumin, pepper, and salt and simmer for another 30 minutes. Puree the soup in a blender, food processor, or food mill. Serve hot, garnished with chopped egg and minced scallions.

CHICKEN STOCK

2 pounds chicken scraps,
including some bones
1 large onion, peeled and
stuck with 3 or 4 whole
cloves
1 large clove garlic, peeled
2 ribs celery, halved
crosswise, with leaves if
available
1 or 2 carrots, cut into
chunks

1 bay leaf
2 or more parsley sprigs or 1
tablespoon dried parsley
flakes
1 teaspoon tarragon
1/2 teaspoon thyme
1/2 teaspoon dill weed
salt to taste
12 peppercorns or 1/4 -1/2
teaspoon freshly ground
black pepper

Food for thought:
To degrease soup,
first spoon as
much grease as
possible from the
top. Open a paper
towel and float it
across the surface
of the liquid
to absorb any
remaining grease.

Place all ingredients in a large pot, fill to cover with cold water. Bring the liquid to a boil, reduce the heat, partially cover the pot, and simmer the stock for at least one hour. The longer the stock cooks, the richer it will become. Pour the stock through a fine strainer, sieve, or cheesecloth into a fat-separating measuring cup, or into a large bowl. Decant the fat-free broth (if using the fat skimmer) into storage containers or refrigerate the bowl of stock until the fat hardens enough for easy removal.

Note: Once the stock is prepared, freeze it into several types of containers: ice-cube trays, 1 and 2 cup plastic tubs and 1 quart containers. This delicious stock is wonderful to have on hand for great soups and sauces.

STORM SOUP

4 cups chicken broth
2/3 cup dried green split peas
1 medium onion, chopped
2 cups chopped cooked ham
(bone if you have it)

1/4 teaspoon salt
1/4 teaspoon pepper
3 medium Idaho potatoes,
diced
3 medium carrots, sliced

Combine first six ingredients in heavy kettle. Place over high heat and boil 5 minutes; cover and simmer one hour stirring occasionally. Remove ham bone , then add potatoes and carrots and continue to simmer for 20 minutes or until vegetables are done.

CHUNKY HAM & POTATO CHOWDER

½ cup sliced leek or coarsely chopped onion
1 tablespoon margarine
2 teaspoons fresh thyme or ½ teaspoon dried thyme
¼ teaspoon salt
¼ teaspoon pepper
3 cups milk

1½ cups chopped fully cooked ham
1½ cups chopped fully cooked turkey
1 cup instant potato buds
¼ cup loosely packed torn fresh basil
cracked black pepper

In 2 quart saucepan, cook leek in hot margarine until tender. Stir in fresh thyme, salt and pepper. Add milk. Cook until heated through. Stir in ham, turkey, potato buds and basil. Add more milk if it's too thick. Sprinkle each serving with cracked pepper.

CREAM OF TOMATO SOUP

4 tablespoons butter
1 medium onion, finely chopped
1 carrot, finely chopped
4 cups chicken stock
1 bay leaf
3 35-ounce cans of whole peeled tomatoes, drained, seeded, and chopped or 8 ripe tomatoes, peeled, seeded and chopped.

2 teaspoons salt
1 teaspoon Worcestershire sauce
½ teaspoon minced garlic
1 tablespoon fresh chopped dill
1 cup light cream
1 cup grated Monterey Jack cheese

In a large saucepan melt butter and sauté onion and carrot until soft; 8-10 minutes. Add stock, bay leaf, tomatoes, salt, Worcestershire sauce and garlic and cook over low heat for 1½-2 hours. Remove bay leaf and add dill and cream. In a blender, blend soup in small batches. Reheat if needed and divide among bowls, garnish with cheese.

"The sensitive periods must be recognized, and the child provided with proper assistance to learn each skill at the the proper time."
— Maria Montessori

MINESTRONE SOUP

3 medium carrots, cleaned and coarsely chopped
3 stalks celery, coarsely chopped
2 medium onions, chopped
1 large potato, pared and cut into 3/4" cubes
1/4 pound green beans, cut into 1" pieces
2 medium zucchini, cut into 1/2" cubes
1/2 pound cabbage, coarsely shredded
1 medium clove garlic, minced

1/3 cup olive oil
3 tablespoons butter
31/2 cups beef broth
11/2 cups water
1 28-ounce can Italian plum tomatoes
1/2 teaspoon salt
1/2 teaspoon dried basil
1/4 teaspoon pepper
1/4 teaspoon dried rosemary
1 bay leaf
1 16-ounce can cannellini beans

Don't let the list of ingredients fool you. This soup is easy to make and has a wonderful flavor. Because of the potato it doesn't freeze very well. Use a small pasta such as orzo if freezing.

In a 5 quart Dutch oven, heat oil and butter over medium heat. Add onions; sauté stirring occasionally until soft and golden (6-8 minutes). Add carrots and potatoes; sauté 5 minutes more. Stir in celery and green beans sauté 5 minutes. Stir in zucchini; sauté 3 minutes. Stir in cabbage and garlic; cook one minute. Add broth, water and liquid from tomatoes to pan. Coarsely chop tomatoes and add to pan. Stir in salt, pepper, basil, rosemary and bay leaf. Heat to boiling and reduce heat to low. Simmer covered, stirring occasionally for 11/2 hours. Rinse and drain beans; add to soup. Cook uncovered over low-medium heat, stirring occasionally until soup is thick, about 30-40 minutes more. Remove bay leaf. Serve with freshly ground Parmesan cheese.

BAKED MINESTRONE

1 1/2 pounds lean beef for stew, cut into cubes
1 cup coarsely chopped onion
2 cloves crushed garlic
1 teaspoon salt
1/4 teaspoon pepper
2 tablespoons olive oil
3 10-ounce cans condensed beef broth
2 soup cans water
1 1/2 teaspoons Italian seasoning
1 16-ounce can tomatoes (include liquid)
1 15 1/4-ounce can kidney beans (include liquid)
1 1/2 cups thinly sliced carrots
1 cup small seashell macaroni, uncooked
2 cups sliced zucchini
grated Parmesan cheese

Preheat oven to 400°. Mix beef, onion, garlic, salt and pepper in a large ovenproof pot. Add olive oil and stir to coat meat evenly. Bake at 400° until meat is browned, stirring once. Turn oven down to 350°. Add broth, water and seasonings to meat, stir. Cover and cook one hour or until meat is tender. Stir in tomatoes, kidney beans, carrots and macaroni. Put sliced zucchini on top. Cover and bake 30-40 minutes until carrots are tender. Serve with grated cheese.

DAD'S TORTELLINI SOUP

2 28-ounce cans crushed tomatoes
3 16-ounce cans beef broth
3 16-ounce cans water
3 carrots, sliced
1/2 cabbage, shredded
3 stalks celery, sliced
2 potatoes, cubed
1 tablespoon dried fennel
1 tablespoon dried oregano
1 teaspoon dried basil
salt and pepper

1 19-ounce can white kidney beans
1 pound cheese tortellini
1 pound sweet Italian sausage (boil separately and then cut into pieces)

Combine first set of ingredients in a large pot. Simmer 2 hours. Then add kidney beans, tortellini and sausage and continue to simmer until tortellini is cooked.

WEDDING SOUP

**1 pound ground meat
  (sirloin, beef, or turkey)**
fresh parsley
1-3 cloves garlic, minced
salt and pepper

**1 8-ounce box frozen
  chopped spinach**
2 cups steamed rice
8-12 cups broth

In a large mixing bowl combine meat, parsley, garlic, salt and pepper to form meatballs; broil or sauté, then drain on paper towels. In Dutch oven or similar, mix broth, spinach and rice. Cook over medium heat until mixture comes to a boil. Lower heat, add the meatballs, simmer for 5 minutes, then serve.

IN A PICKLE CHILI

2 pounds ground chuck
1 large onion
2 tablespoons chopped garlic
2 cans kidney beans
2 cans black beans

3 dill pickles, chopped
3 jalapeño peppers, chopped
2 cans diced tomatoes
$1/2$ pound sliced mushrooms

Sauté beef, onion and garlic until meat is cooked. Add the rest of the ingredients and simmer 15-20 minutes. Serve with garlic bread, rice and something cold to drink.

I'M SPEECHLESS CHILI

3 tablespoons olive oil
1 medium pepper
2 medium onions
4 garlic cloves, diced
2 pounds ground beef
1 envelope Old El Paso
   Taco Seasoning
2 teaspoons ground cayenne
   pepper
pinch cloves

pinch cinnamon
1 tablespoon Tabasco
1/2 jar salsa
1 can black beans
1 can hot chili beans
1 can cannellini beans
1 can corn
1 can chunk style tomatoes
3 tablespoons chopped
   jalapeños

Sauté pepper, onions, and garlic in olive oil. Brown ground beef. Stir in next 6 ingredients. Drain and then add the beans and corn. Add the tomatoes and jalapeños. Cook over low heat for 2 hours. (hot hot hot)!

WHITE TURKEY CHILI

1 1/2 cups coarsely chopped
   onion
2 garlic cloves, minced
1 tablespoon olive oil
1 jalapeño, minced
1 4-ounce can minced mild
   green chilies
1 teaspoon ground cumin
1/2 teaspoon dried oregano
1/4 teaspoon cayenne pepper
1/4 teaspoon salt

1 cup reduced sodium
   chicken stock
1 19-ounce can white kidney
   beans (cannellini), drained
   and rinsed
2 cups cooked turkey, cut
   into 1/2" cubes
1/4 cup coarsely chopped
   fresh cilantro
1/2 cup grated reduced-fat
   Monterey Jack cheese

In 3 quart saucepan over medium-high heat, sauté onions and garlic in oil for 5 minutes or until onion is tender. Add jalapeño, chilies, cumin, oregano, cayenne pepper and salt. Cook one minute. Stir in stock, beans, and turkey. Bring to boil, reduce heat and simmer, uncovered, 20 to 25 minutes or until slightly thickened. Stir in cilantro. To serve, ladle into bowls and top each with 2 tablespoons cheese.

Food for thought: To easily remove a garlic clove from liquid mixture, insert a wooden toothpick into the garlic bud before placing it into the sauce or stew...when you're ready to remove the garlic just pull out the toothpick.

CHILI FOR A CROWD

Serves 35 to 40

Great with salad and cornbread for a Super Bowl party. This recipe is tasty and worth the effort!

1/2 cup olive oil
1 3/4 pounds onion, coarsely chopped
2 pounds sweet Italian sausage (removed from casing and crumbled)
8 pounds ground chuck
1 1/2 tablespoons black pepper
2 12-ounce cans tomato paste
3 tablespoons minced garlic
3 ounces ground cumin or to taste
4 ounces plain chili powder or to taste
1/2 cup Dijon mustard
4 tablespoons salt (optional)

4 tablespoons dried basil
4 tablespoons dried oregano
5 2-pound 3-ounce cans peeled plum tomatoes
1/2 cup burgundy
1/4 cup lemon juice
1/2 cup chopped dill (or 1/4 cup dried dill)
1/2 cup chopped Italian parsley
3 16-ounce cans dark kidney beans, drained
scallions for garnish
cheddar cheese for garnish
black olives for garnish
sour cream for garnish

Heat olive oil in large kettle. Add onions and cook on low heat until tender and translucent. Crumble sausage meat and chuck into kettle and brown, spooning out as much excess fat as possible. Over low heat, stir in black pepper, tomato paste, garlic, cumin, chili powder, mustard, salt, basil and oregano. Drain tomatoes and coarsely chop, put in kettle, add burgundy, lemon juice, dill, parsley and drained beans. Stir well and simmer 30-60 minutes, or longer. Taste and correct seasonings. Serve immediately with scallions, cheddar cheese, black olives and sour cream as garnish. Recipe can be halved or even quartered.

VEGGIES

VEGETABLES

WHO NEEDS DESSERT...
BROCCOLI CASSEROLE

1 large bunch fresh broccoli, chopped or 2 10-ounce packages frozen chopped broccoli
3 eggs, slightly beaten

1 12-ounce cottage cheese
1 cup grated cheddar cheese
1 tablespoon flour
2 teaspoons salt
dash of pepper

If using frozen broccoli thaw broccoli. DO NOT COOK. If using fresh broccoli, rinse and blanch. Press out water with paper towel. Combine eggs, both cheeses, flour, salt and pepper. Add broccoli and mix well. Bake in greased casserole at 350° for 30-40 minutes.

PARMESAN BROCCOLI PUREE
So easy, it takes longer to write it than to make it.

1 large bunch fresh broccoli
2-3 tablespoons fresh grated Parmesan cheese

dash of nutmeg

Rinse broccoli and coarsely chop florets (add stems if you wish), boil until soft, drain. Place broccoli in a blender or food processor with steel blade; purée broccoli to desired consistency. Stir in Parmesan cheese and nutmeg to taste. This makes a nice accompaniment to chicken dishes and is also good over pasta.

Although broccoli is available year round, peak season is October-April. Look for a deep strong green or green with purple color with buds tightly closed and crisp leaves.

VIDALIA ONION CASSEROLE

*Vidalia onions,
hailing from
nearby Vidalia,
Georgia, are
famous on Hilton
Head not just for
their sweet,
succulent taste.
For years,
Islanders
officially
welcomed
warmer weather
only when
"The Onion Man"
reappeared.
Every April,
he returned to
park his bright
orange school
bus-- packed full
of vidalia onions–
on a vacant lot
near Sea Pines
Circle, to sit
and sell these
pungent bulbs all
summer long.*

4 jumbo Vidalias
1/2 cup margarine
5 ounces evaporated milk
3 medium eggs
1 stack Ritz crackers

**1 1/2 cup grated longhorn/colby
cheese**
salt and pepper to taste
3 tablespoons margarine

Preheat oven to 375°. Peel, wash and slice onions. In a large pot boil onions until tender, about 5 minutes. Drain water, return onions to pot and add margarine. When margarine has melted mix in milk and eggs and 1 cup of cheese. In a large bowl, crush Ritz crackers–set aside 1/4 cup for topping. When cheese has melted remove onion mixture from heat and stir into Ritz crackers. Pour onion/Ritz mixture into casserole dish and bake for 35 minutes. Sprinkle 1/2 cup of cheese and 1/4 cup of cracker crumbs and dot with butter. Return to oven for 2-5 minutes, just long enough for cheese and butter to melt.

GARLIC ROASTED CRUNCHY VEGETABLES

**24 small unpeeled garlic
cloves**
1 tablespoon olive oil
**3/4 pound broccoli, cut into
bite sized pieces**
**3/4 pound baby carrots,
peeled and trimmed**

1 tablespoon sugar
3 tablespoons butter
2 tablespoons fresh parsley
salt and pepper to taste

Preheat oven to 275°. Add garlic to 2 cups boiling water, boil 3 minutes then drain. Peel and trim garlic root ends. Heat oil in a small oven-proof skillet, add garlic cloves and toss. Cover loosely with foil, bake 30 minutes, stirring once. Remove foil. Bake 10 minutes more, until tender. Remove from oven and set aside. In a microwave safe container with lid, cook broccoli in two tablespoons of water on high heat for 5 minutes. Drain and set aside. Add sugar and carrots to 3 cups boiling water with 1/2 teaspoon salt. Boil until just tender, approximately 10 minutes. Drain and set aside. When ready to serve, melt butter in a large heavy skillet. Add vegetables (garlic, broccoli and carrots) to pan, heat through, tossing gently. Sprinkle with parsley, salt and pepper to taste.

SAUTÉ OF
JULIENNED GARDEN VEGETABLES

4 medium carrots, peeled
  and julienned
4 medium stalks celery,
  julienned
2 tablespoons unsalted butter
2 tablespoons oil
1 medium Vidalia onion,
  thinly sliced

3 medium zucchini,
  julienned
1 medium clove garlic,
  minced
lemon pepper to taste
1 tablespoon chopped
  parsley

Immerse carrots in pan of boiling water and boil one minute. Drain and set aside. Immerse celery in pan of boiling water and boil 30 seconds. Drain and set aside. Heat butter and oil in large skillet until hot. Add onion and sauté over medium heat for 3-5 minutes or until soft but not brown. Add carrots and celery and continue sautéing another minute. Add zucchini and sauté another 2 minutes or until cooked but not soft. Add garlic, lemon pepper and parsley. Mix well, add salt to taste and serve immediately.

SPINACH MADELEINE

2 packages frozen, chopped
  spinach
4 tablespoons butter
2 tablespoons flour
2 tablespoons chopped onion
1 clove minced garlic
1/2 cup evaporated milk
1/2 cup spinach cooking liquid

1/2 teaspoon black pepper
1/2 to1 teaspoon salt
3/4 cups grated cheddar or
  Monterey Jack with
  jalapeño cheese
1 teaspoon Worcestershire
  sauce

Cook spinach according to package directions. Drain and reserve liquid. Melt butter in saucepan over low heat. Add flour to butter, stirring until blended and smooth, but not brown. Add onion and garlic and continue to cook until soft. Add spinach liquid and evaporated milk slowly, stirring constantly to avoid lumps. Cook until smooth and thick; continue stirring. Add seasonings and cheese and stir until melted. Combine with cooked spinach. Serve immediately.

Note: This can be made a day ahead; the flavors blend nicely if left refrigerated overnight.

ASPARAGUS & PEA CASSEROLE

Due to it's "crown-like" appearance, asparagus is known in culinary circles as the "King of Vegetables".

1 pound green asparagus steamed/blanched
1 can peas, drained
4 hard boiled eggs, sliced
1/2 cup grated sharp cheddar cheese

1 can cream of mushroom soup
1/2 cup slivered almonds, toasted
2 tablespoons saltine cracker crumbs buttered

Preheat oven to 350°. In casserole, mix asparagus and peas alternately with sliced eggs. In a small saucepan, heat soup, stir in cheese, heat until melted. Pour cheese sauce over asparagus and peas. Top with almonds and buttered cracker crumbs. Bake 35-45 minutes.

GREEN PEAS WITH PINE NUTS & ROSEMARY

2 10-ounce packages of frozen peas, thawed or fresh 3 1/2 cups shelled green peas
3 green onions
1/2 cup chicken stock
1/2 teaspoon sugar

3 tablespoons unsalted butter
3/4 cup pine nuts
1 tablespoon chopped fresh rosemary (or 1 teaspoon crushed dried)
salt and pepper to taste

Trim the scallions, leaving 2 inches of green stem. Cut them into 1/2 inch pieces. Place chicken stock in a medium sized saucepan over medium heat. Add sugar and scallions, and bring the stock to a simmer. Add peas, cooking approximately 3 minutes (5-8 minutes longer if using fresh peas). Drain the vegetables and set aside. Melt butter in a large heavy skillet over medium heat. When the butter is hot, add pine nuts and cook, stirring constantly, until golden, approximately 2-3 minutes. Stir in rosemary and cook one minute. Add peas and cook, stirring until hot, 2-3 minutes. Season to taste.

CARROTS IN ORANGE-GINGER SAUCE

24 baby carrots
juice of 4 oranges
2 teaspoons grated orange
  rind
2 teaspoons grated fresh
  ginger

2 teaspoons flour
1/2 teaspoon salt
4 tablespoons butter

Wash carrots, and trim ends. Cut carrots lengthwise into four strips. Boil carrot strips until just tender. Remove from heat but do not drain. In another pan whisk together remaining ingredients, except butter, over medium heat until thickened. Add butter and cook until melted. Drain carrots. Put carrots in a bowl pour sauce over carrots, stir to coat. Keep carrots in a warm oven until ready to serve.

CRISPY EGGPLANT PESTO

large eggplant

1/2-1 cup pesto

PESTO:
3 cups loosely packed fresh
  basil leaves
1/3 cup pine nuts
1/2 cup grated Parmesan
  cheese

3 garlic cloves, coarsely
  chopped
1/2 cup olive oil
salt and ground black pepper
  to taste

For Pesto: In a food processor or blender combine all ingredients except oil. When well chopped, add the oil in a thin stream to form a smooth paste. Pesto will keep refrigerated for 1 week. If freezing pesto, store in plastic bags or in ice cube trays. Whirl frozen thawed pesto in the blender briefly to improve it's texture.

Preheat oven to 400°. Peel and slice eggplant 1/4" thick. Spread pesto on both sides of eggplant slices. Place on ungreased cookie sheet. Bake 10-15 minutes, turn over when golden brown on bottom. Cook 5-10 minutes more. Eggplant is done when lightly crisp. Great served with pasta dishes.

EGGPLANT PARMIGIANA

2 medium eggplants
1 cup flour
1 egg beaten
salt and pepper to taste
olive oil

2 cups spaghetti or
 marinara sauce
1/2 pound whole milk
 mozzarella cheese, grated
1/2 cup Parmesan cheese,
 grated

Peel eggplants and slice 1/3" thick. Bring a large pot of water to a boil, put in eggplant slices, cover pot, and cook 1 minute. Immediately drain in a colander and pat dry. Dredge slices in flour seasoned with salt and pepper then dip in egg. Put a thin film of olive oil in a large frying pan. Sauté slices over medium-high heat until pale gold on each side. Add more olive oil to pan as needed. Remove to a plate covered in paper towels to drain.

Preheat oven to 350°. Coat a large shallow casserole lightly with olive oil. Spread some tomato sauce in the bottom, then make layers of eggplant, tomato sauce, mozzarella, and Parmesan cheese. Dribble a little olive oil over the top layer of Parmesan cheese and bake uncovered 20-30 minutes, or until hot and bubbly. Serve hot or warm.

EGGPLANT CASSEROLE

1 small eggplant
1 cup flour
1 egg, beaten
1 cup cornmeal
1 cup olive oil
1/2 cup sliced green peppers
1 cup sliced mushrooms

1 garlic clove, chopped
2 tablespoons basil
1 teaspoon parsley
2 cups cottage cheese
 (drained)
1 8-ounce can chopped
 tomatoes (reserve liquid)

Preheat oven 325°. Peel eggplant and cut into 1/4" slices. Discard stem and end. Dredge eggplant slices in the following order: flour, egg, cornmeal. Heat olive oil in deep frying pan. Drop 3 or 4 slices at a time into hot olive oil. Fry until golden. Drain on paper towels. Layer in a 9 x 12" glass pan in the following order: fried eggplant, green pepper, mushrooms, garlic, basil and parsley. Spread cottage cheese over eggplant, vegetable mixture. Top with chopped tomatoes. Bake until bubbly, about 35 minutes. Serve with spinach pasta.

LEMON DILL GREEN BEANS

1 pound fresh green beans   fresh dill
2 lemons

Put a large pot of water on to boil. Rinse and pinch stem ends leaving beans whole. Plunge into boiling water and cook for 8 minutes. While beans are boiling, juice 2 lemons. Beans will be tender-crisp and still bright green. Drain and give a quick rinse with cold water. Pour lemon juice over your lovely green, green beans and shake lots and lots of dill, or a generous handful of fresh chopped dill. Toss and serve. Wow! Incredible flavor. Refrigerate leftover lemon dill beans for a picnic, yummy finger food.

ROASTED GREEN BEANS

1 pound fresh green beans   fresh lemon juice
1 1/2 tablespoons olive oil   pepper to taste

Preheat oven to 500°. Trim the beans, spread on a cookie sheet, drizzle with oil and bake for 6-8 minutes until tender, turning them occasionally. Remove to serving dish, squeeze lemon juice over them, and sprinkle pepper to taste.

Food for thought: To retain their color, flavor and nutrients, green beans should be blanched.

GREEN BEANS ALMANDINE

pound fresh green beans,   1/4 cup butter or margarine
washed and tips removed   1/2 teaspoon salt
2-ounce package slivered   juice of 1/2 lemon
almonds

Cook beans in small amount of water until tender. Drain. With two sharp knives, cut beans into very thin shreds. In small skillet, melt butter. Add almonds and toss. Cook until crisp and lightly browned (be careful, almonds burn easily.) Remove from heat. Add salt and lemon juice. Pour mixture over hot cooked beans.

GREEN BEANS IN ONION & GARLIC SAUCE

1 pound green beans
1 tablespoon soy sauce
1 teaspoon sugar
1 tablespoon dry sherry or
  white wine
1 small chicken bouillon
  cube

2/3 cup chicken broth
1 tablespoon oil
2 tablespoons butter
4-6 cloves minced garlic
2 scallions, chopped
2 tablespoons minced ginger

Mix soy, sugar and sherry. Set aside. In large saucepan, dissolve bouillon in chicken broth over high heat. Add the beans. Simmer until nearly all liquid has evaporated, 5-7 minutes, stirring constantly. Drain beans. Set aside. In wok or skillet, heat oil and butter. Add garlic, scallions, ginger. Stir fry about 30 seconds until just softened. Add the beans and toss until coated. Sprinkle soy sauce mixture over beans and stir fry another minute. Serve immediately.

YELLOW SQUASH CASSEROLE

5-6 medium yellow squash,
  sliced
1/4 green pepper, chopped
1 small onion, chopped
1/2 cup melted butter

1/2 cup mayonnaise
1/2 cup grated Parmesan
  cheese
1/2 cup plain bread crumbs
1 egg

Preheat oven to 350°. Boil onion and green pepper until tender. Drain. Mix squash, peppers, onions and other ingredients together. Mix well. Pour into casserole dish and bake for 45 minutes.

"The senses, being the explorers of the world, open the way to knowledge..."
— Maria Montessori

TOMATO & ARTICHOKE CASSEROLE

1 28-ounce can whole
  tomatoes
1 14-ounce can artichoke
  hearts
1/2 cup chopped onion
2 tablespoons shallots

1/2 cup butter
1/2 teaspoon basil
2 teaspoons sugar
salt and pepper to taste

Preheat oven to 325°. Grease casserole dish. Drain and
quarter tomatoes and artichokes. Sauté onions and shallots in
butter until tender. Add tomatoes, artichokes and basil. Heat
2-3 minutes. Stirring gently, add sugar, salt and pepper.
Place in casserole dish. Bake 10-15 minutes.

THE DEFINITIVE
FRIED GREEN TOMATO

4-6 green tomatoes
1 cup cornmeal
1 teaspoon cayenne pepper
  (or to taste)

1 teaspoon salt
1/2 teaspoon Lawry's
  seasoned salt
vegetable oil for frying

Slice firm green tomatoes 1/8" thick. Heat oil in skillet until
bubbles form. Mix cornmeal and spices in large bowl. Dredge
tomatoes in cornmeal and spice mixture. Fry until crust on
tomatoes is golden brown. Drain on paper towels. Serve
immediately. Garnish with a dollop of sour cream.

BUNNY'S CARROT PUDDING

1 pound cooked carrots	1 teaspoon vanilla
3 eggs	1/4 cup butter, melted
1/3 cup sugar	1/3 teaspoon cinnamon
3 tablespoons flour	nutmeg to taste

TOPPING:

1/3-1/2 cup crushed cornflakes (or walnuts)	2 tablespoons butter, softened
3 tablespoons brown sugar	

Preheat oven to 350°. Mix carrots and eggs in blender (not food processor). Add all other ingredients and blend again. Put into 1 1/2 quart souffle pan. Bake for 40 minutes.

While carrot pudding is baking combine topping ingredients. Spread topping over carrot pudding and cook 5-10 minutes more.

SAN FRANCISCO TOMATO PUDDING

1/2 teaspoon salt	3/4 cup butter
2 1/2 cups tomato puree	3 cups 1" cubes sourdough bread
1 1/4 cups brown sugar	
1/4 cup boiling water	

Preheat oven to 375°. In a medium sized saucepan combine the salt, tomato puree, brown sugar and boiling water. Place the pan over moderate heat and bring the ingredients to a boil. Let boil for 5 minutes, stirring occasionally. Meanwhile, melt the butter in a small saucepan and keep both the tomato mixture and the butter warm while proceeding with the recipe.

Place the bread cubes in a buttered 9" square pan and pour the hot melted butter over them, distributing it evenly. Pour the hot tomato mixture evenly over the buttered bread cubes. Bake for 45 minutes.

GRAINS
PASTA·RICE·POTATOES

GRAINS

FRESH PASTA WITH SMOKED SALMON, DILL & GOLDEN CAVIAR

SAUCE:

1 cup whipping cream
2 tablespoons cream cheese, softened
1 tablespoon unsalted butter

1/4 teaspoon salt
fresh cracked black pepper, to taste

PASTA:

1 tablespoon oil
1 teaspoon salt
3/4 pound fettuccine, preferably fresh
1/4 pound smoked salmon cut into small pieces

2 tablespoons finely chopped fresh dill
1 1/2-ounces golden caviar
dill sprigs

In a small saucepan heat cream over moderately high heat until reduced to 3/4 cup. Add cream cheese and whisk until slightly thickened. Add butter and continue cooking one minute. Add salt and pepper.

Meanwhile, to a large pot of boiling water add oil and salt. Add pasta and cook over high heat until al dente. Drain well. Place in large pasta serving dish or medium bowl. Add cream sauce to pasta. Sprinkle smoked salmon, dill and 1/3 of caviar over pasta and toss gently but thoroughly. Divide among plates and garnish with remaining caviar and dill sprigs. Serve immediately.

PASTA WITH CHICKEN, BROCCOLI & SUNDRIED TOMATOES

Food for thought:
Sundried
tomatoes add a
rich intense flavor
to soups,
sandwiches,
salads and
sauces.

1/4 cup olive oil
2 cloves garlic, minced
1/2 pound boneless chicken breasts, cut in strips
1 1/2 cups fresh broccoli florets
3/4 cup oil packed sundried tomatoes, drained and sliced

1 teaspoon dried basil
pinch of crushed red pepper flakes
salt and pepper to taste
1/4 cup dry white wine
3/4 cup chicken broth
1 tablespoon butter
1/2 pound bow-tie pasta
grated Parmesan cheese

In large skillet heat oil over medium heat; sauté garlic for 1 minute. Add chicken and sauté until almost thoroughly cooked (7-10 minutes), add broccoli and sauté until crisp tender, add sundried tomatoes, basil, red pepper, salt and pepper. Next add the wine, then add chicken broth and butter, stir until combined. Cook 3-5 minutes. Toss with freshly cooked pasta. Sprinkle with Parmesan cheese. For vegetarians use   vegetable broth and substitute more broccoli or onions for chicken.

FETTUCCINE WITH SPINACH GORGONZOLA & WALNUTS

2 tablespoons olive or sesame oil
1 large clove garlic, minced
2 cups torn, stemmed, fresh spinach
1/2 cup (2 ounces) crumbled Gorgonzola cheese

1/4 cup coarsely chopped walnuts
6 ounces hot, cooked fettuccine
fresh ground white pepper

Heat olive oil in large skillet. Add garlic and cook over low heat 5 minutes. Add spinach and cook over medium heat until tender, about 5 minutes, stirring frequently. Stir in cheese and nuts. Add cooked fettuccine and toss well to melt cheese into spinach and pasta. Season well with white pepper. Serve with hot crusty bread.

PASTA WITH VODKA

1 pound penne pasta
4 tablespoons butter
2/3 cup vodka
1/4 teaspoon hot red pepper flakes or more to taste
1 16-ounce can Italian plum tomatoes, drained, seeded and pureed

3/4 cup heavy cream
1/2 teaspoon salt
3/4 cup freshly grated Parmesan cheese

Cook penne until tender but still firm. Melt butter in large skillet over moderate heat. Add vodka and hot pepper and simmer for two minutes. Add pureed tomatoes and cream and simmer for 5 minutes longer. Season with salt. Drain pasta and put into pan with hot sauce. Reduce heat and add cheese. Serve at once.

PENNE IN SPICY TOMATO SAUCE

1 pound penne pasta
1 tablespoon olive oil
3 cloves garlic chopped
1/2 teaspoon crushed red pepper flakes
4 14-ounce cans diced tomatoes, drained

1 cup fresh grated Pecorino Romano cheese
1/4 cup chopped fresh parsley or 2 tablespoons dry parsley

Cook penne al dente. Heat oil with garlic and red pepper for one minute. Add tomatoes and simmer for about 5-10 minutes. Add salt and pepper to taste. Add cooked pasta to sauce and heat on high, stirring until bubbly. Remove from heat and add cheese and parsley. Toss and serve immediately.

Food for thought: To easily grate Parmesan and other hard cheeses, cut the cheese into 1 inch cubes and place them in a blender jar. Turn the blender on high speed for 30 seconds or until all of the cheese cube is grated. Grate in small amounts.

JANE'S LINGUINE WITH CHERRY TOMATOES & BASIL

25-30 cherry tomatoes, cut in quarters or half
1/2 pound Brie
1/2 pound mozzarella
1 cup fresh basil leaves chopped (or 4 tablespoons dry basil)
3 garlic cloves, peeled and finely minced

1/3 cup olive oil
2 1/2 teaspoons salt
1/2 teaspoon ground black pepper
1 1/2 pounds linguine or fettuccine
1/2 cup freshly grated Parmesan cheese.

Cook linguine for 8-10 minutes. Meanwhile, heat olive oil in microwave for 1-2 minutes. Then combine tomatoes, cheeses, basil, garlic, heated olive oil, salt and pepper. Drain pasta and toss with tomato mixture. Add Parmesan to taste.

ROTINI WITH VESUVIUS SAUCE

You can make this with spaghetti but the macaroni is much easier for children to manage.

1 pound rotini or shells macaroni
1 tablespoon olive oil
2 14-ounce Italian plum tomatoes, chopped

1 teaspoon dried oregano
salt
Parmesan & mozzarella to taste

Heat the oil in a saucepan and add the chopped tomatoes with their juice. Add the oregano and salt to taste and cook rapidly for 20 minutes. While the sauce is cooking, cook the macaroni until firm. When the macaroni is ready, drain and put into a casserole or pan with a cover. Stir in the tomato sauce, sprinkle with Parmesan and mozzarella cheeses. Cover and leave for about 3 minutes so that the mozzarella begins to melt and look like streams of molten lava. Serve hot.

GRANDMOTHER'S MACARONI & CHEESE

1 cup small elbow macaroni
1/2 teaspoon salt
1/2 pound cheddar cheese, grated
3 eggs

1 cup milk
salt and pepper to taste
paprika
bread crumbs

Preheat oven to 350°. Cook macaroni in about 1 1/2 quarts water and 1/2 teaspoon salt for about 10 minutes; drain. Put part of macaroni in a buttered dish. Add part of cheese. Layer macaroni and cheese. In separate bowl beat 3 eggs and mix in milk; add salt and pepper to taste. Pour milk and eggs over macaroni and cheese. Sprinkle bread crumbs and paprika on top. Bake for 30 minutes.

ANGEL IN PARADISE PASTA

1 whole head of garlic
olive oil
2 tablespoons butter
salt to taste
4 green onions, minced with part of tops

1/4 cup minced parsley
1 pound angel hair pasta
1/4 cup grated Parmesan cheese

Preheat oven to 350°. Separate cloves from the head of garlic and place on a sheet of foil. Sprinkle with a little olive oil and turn to coat them, then fold up in foil to make a secure packet. Bake 30-45 minutes or until cloves are completely soft. Remove from oven and cool to room temperature. Press out garlic "meat" from garlic cloves into a small bowl. Mash thoroughly with butter, add salt to taste, then stir in onions and parsley. Cook pasta al dente. Drain and put back into the pot with the garlic mixture. Toss well with fork and sprinkle with Parmesan cheese.

Garlic can be cooked at any time you have something in the oven, and like baked potatoes can be cooked at any temperature. It can then be stored in the refrigerator in its packet until you need it.

FETTUCCINE ALFREDO WITH PEAS & ARTICHOKES

1 1/2 cups half and half
3 tablespoons butter
1/2 teaspoon salt
1 cup grated Parmesan cheese
dash of nutmeg

salt and pepper to taste
1 small package frozen peas
1 16-ounce can artichoke hearts, slightly chopped
1 16-ounce package fettuccine

Cook pasta. While pasta is cooking , blend butter, cream, salt and pepper in pan over medium-low heat. Simmer for 5 minutes to thicken. Add nutmeg, peas and artichokes; simmer until bubbly for 5 minutes more. Remove from heat. Drain pasta when cooked al dente. Toss pasta with sauce and add Parmesan cheese.

"What we have to learn to do we learn by doing..."
– Aristotle

BAKED RIGATONI WITH MOZZARELLA

1 15-ounce can diced tomatoes with juice
1 tablespoon olive oil
1 medium onion, finely chopped
1 8-ounce can tomato sauce
3 cloves minced garlic
1/2 teaspoon dried oregano
1 teaspoon dried basil

1/4 teaspoon crushed fennel seeds
1/2 teaspoon sugar
1/8 teaspoon black pepper
8 ounces rigatoni or ziti, cooked and drained
1 cup grated mozzarella
2 tablespoons grated Parmesan cheese

Preheat oven to 375°. Heat the olive oil in a skillet, add the onion and garlic and sauté until soft. Add the tomatoes, tomato sauce, oregano, basil, fennel seeds, and pepper; bring to a boil. Reduce the heat to low and simmer, uncovered, for 10 minutes, stirring often, until the sauce has thickened slightly. Place the cooked pasta in a shallow, ungreased 1 1/2 quart casserole. Cover with the sauce, and sprinkle with the mozzarella and Parmesan cheese. Bake uncovered for 30-35 minutes, or until bubbly and golden. Let stand for 5 minutes before serving.

SPINACH LASAGNA

1 jar Paul Newman's
 Spaghetti Sauce
1 can stewed tomatoes,
 undrained
1/2 green bell pepper
1/2 red bell pepper
1 red onion
1 clove garlic, minced
2 to 4 tablespoons olive oil
1 tablespoon basil

1 teaspoon sugar
2 eggs, beaten
1 16-ounce ricotta cheese
2 packages frozen chopped
 spinach
1 cup fresh grated Parmesan
 cheese
1 package lasagna noodles
4 cups grated mozzarella
 cheese

Preheat oven to 350°. Combine Paul Newman sauce with
stewed tomatoes. Chop peppers and onion, then in a medium
pan, sauté peppers and onions in olive oil until tender. Add
sauce, basil and sugar. Stir and allow to simmer over low heat.
Meanwhile assemble the rest of the ingredients. In a large
mixing bowl combine beaten eggs, ricotta, thawed and
drained spinach and 1/2 of the Parmesan cheese. Spread 1 1/3
cup tomato mixture in a large greased baking dish.

Layer half of partially cooked lasagna noodles, [Note: don't
cook the noodles more than 5 or 6 minutes before assembling
with other ingredients or you'll have a "tough" finished product,] spinach mixture, mozzarella and tomato. Repeat, ending
with tomato sauce. Top with remaining Parmesan. Cover tightly with foil and bake at least 1 hour and 10 minutes or until
hot and bubbly throughout. Let stand 10 minutes before serving. Even more flavorful when assembled the day before
serving; allow approximately 20 minutes more cooking time.

*Food for thought:
For a nice
distinguishable
flavor add a dash
of nutmeg to
ricotta cheese in
lasagna recipes.*

PASTA WITH CREAM CHEESE & WALNUTS

1 pound package small shells
  pasta
1¹/₂ tablespoons butter
¹/₂ pound cream cheese

¹/₂ teaspoon sugar
3 tablespoons grated
  Parmesan cheese
¹/₄ cup chopped walnuts

Cook pasta al dente. Drain. In saucepan on medium heat melt butter, add cream cheese and sugar. Melt slowly, stirring often. Stir in pasta, Parmesan cheese and walnuts until blended. Serve warm with sliced tomatoes, and french bread for a quick evening meal.

FREUDIAN NOODLES

1 package wide egg noodles
¹/₂ cup butter, melted
1 8-ounce container cottage
  cheese
1 8-ounce sour cream
¹/₂ cup sugar

1 teaspoon vanilla
1 8-ounce can crushed
  pineapple, drained
4 eggs, beaten

Preheat oven to 325°. Cook noodles until al dente. In separate bowl combine all ingredients except noodles, stir to mix thoroughly; then add noodles. Put mixture in casserole. Cook until bubbly and golden approximately 35-40 minutes.

SWEET PASTA FILLING

1 pound ricotta cheese
1¹/₂ tablespoons sugar
1 egg
parsley
pepper

¹/₈ cup bread crumbs
pinch of cinnamon
grated cheese (Romano or
  Parmesan)

Mix all ingredients together. Prepare pasta shells (18 or so large) or make your own ravioli. Stuff with sweet pasta filling. Spread a thin layer of spaghetti sauce in bottom of 9 x 13" pan. Place shells, open side down, on top. Cover with more sauce. Sprinkle with cheese. Cover with foil and bake at 350° for approximately 35 minutes. This filling can also be used for lasagna.

The pineapple became a symbol of hospitality in colonial times. The wives of ship captains would put a fresh pineapple on the fence post to show that their husbands had arrived home and the family would receive guests.

WILD RICE & APPLES

½ pound wild rice, cooked
½ cup butter, melted
½ cup chopped onion
1 large tart apple, peeled,
   cored and chopped

1 cup fresh bread crumbs
½ cup walnuts chopped
¼ cup fresh orange juice

To cook rice: add rice to 4 cups boiling water and 1 teaspoon salt. Return to boil, stir, reduce to simmer, cover and cook 50 minutes. Uncover and fluff with a fork and continue to simmer 5 more minutes. Drain any excess liquid.

Preheat oven to 325°. Melt butter and use 3 tablespoons of it to lightly sauté onions. Add this mixture to the cooked rice and put in all other ingredients, including the remaining butter. Mix well and put into a 2 quart casserole. Cover and bake 35 minutes. This may be covered and refrigerated, until ready to bake, or stuffed, inside your bird.

SPINACH RICE

2¼ cups water
1 teaspoon salt
1 cup rice
2 eggs beaten
1 can clear chicken broth
4 green onions, chopped

¾ package frozen chopped
   spinach, thawed, rinsed
   and all water squeezed out
1 cup grated cheddar cheese
few pats of butter

Cook rice according to instructions on package. Transfer to a mixing bowl. Add eggs, chicken broth, onions, spinach and stir well to mix. Add ½ of the cheese and the butter pats and stir again. Pour into a 2 quart greased casserole. Add remaining cheese to top. Bake covered for 45 minutes. You can add cooked chopped chicken or turkey to make this a main dish.

Food for thought: Wild rice is not really rice, but a native American aquatic grass.

LEMON PILAF WITH HERBS & ALMONDS

2 tablespoons olive oil
1 medium onion, chopped
2 cloves of garlic, minced
$1/2$ teaspoon turmeric
juice of 1 lemon
2 tablespoons soy sauce
$1/2$ cup chopped fresh basil
$1 1/2$ teaspoons fresh thyme

$1/2$ cup chopped fresh parsley
3 cups cooked brown rice
$1/4$ cup hot water
$2/3$ cup chopped almonds
salt and pepper to taste
1 tablespoon margarine

In a saucepan, sauté the onions and garlic in the olive oil for 5 to 6 minutes, until soft. Stir in the turmeric, lemon juice, and soy sauce. Lower the heat and add the basil, thyme and parsley. Add the rice and mix it well with the seasonings. Drizzle in the hot water. Cover the pot and steam the rice on low heat for 5 minutes. Meanwhile, toast the chopped almonds and place almonds in a single layer on an ungreased baking sheet at 350° for 5 minutes, until lightly browned. To serve, season the pilaf with salt and pepper to taste. Toss with margarine and top with roasted almonds.

SUNNY'S PORTABELLA GRITS

4 portabella mushrooms
6 ounces regular mushrooms
4 tablespoons butter
1 clove garlic, chopped
$3/4$ cup quick grits

2 cups heavy cream
$1/2$ cup grated cheese Swiss,
    Jack and Parmesan)
$1/2$ cup cream cheese
salt and pepper to taste

Wash and slice mushrooms, then sauté in garlic and half of butter. Set aside. Cook grits according to package instructions, substituting cream for water. Add cheeses, butter and stir in sautéed mushrooms. This is a yummy, rich side dish with Southern continental flair.

ORANGE PILAF

3 tablespoons slivered
  almonds
1 cup finely chopped onion
1/4 cup finely chopped green
  pepper
2 tablespoons butter or
  margarine
1 cup long-grain rice

1 cup orange juice
1 cup buttermilk
1/4 teaspoon dried crushed
  oregano
1/2 teaspoon salt
2 oranges, peeled and cut
  into small pieces
paprika

In a 400° oven bake the almonds for 5-10 minutes, shaking the pan occasionally to insure that they brown evenly. In a 10-12 inch skillet, over medium heat, melt the butter, add the onions and green pepper. Sauté until soft, about 5 minutes. Add the rice and brown lightly, stirring constantly, for another 3-5 minutes. Add the orange juice, buttermilk, oregano, and salt. Stir once and bring to a boil over high heat. Cover and reduce heat, simmering for 25 minutes or until it is tender and the liquid is absorbed. Stir the orange pieces and almonds into the cooked rice and heat through. Spoon into a serving bowl and sprinkle with paprika. Serve hot with veal, poultry or lamb.

BROWN RICE WITH CURRANTS & PECANS

1/2 cup coarsely chopped
  pecans
2 tablespoons butter
1/4 cup chopped green
  onions, reserve green ends
  for garnish

1/3 cup dried currants
1 cup brown rice
2 1/2 cups chicken broth

Brown the pecans in the butter, taking care not to burn them. Remove and set aside. Add the white part of the chopped green onions to the butter and cook until soft. In a medium saucepan bring the broth to a boil, add the onions, butter, currants and rice. Cook, covered on very low heat until the liquid is absorbed, about 50 minutes. Toss the browned pecans into the hot rice, garnish with the onion greens. Serve immediately.

Rice was introduced into the Lowcountry as a gift from a sea captain who was forced to dock in Charles Town for repairs on a voyage from Madagascar to England.

Rice grew so well in the coastal wetlands that it was soon the major industry of the area. Eventually the grain became the staple of the local diet and made South Carolina the richest of the 13 Colonies.

COUSCOUS WITH WALNUTS & ARTICHOKE HEARTS

1 cup chicken broth
1 1/2 cups quick cooking
  couscous
1 tablespoon olive oil
1 teaspoon salt
1 14-ounce jar marinated
  artichoke hearts, drained
  and cut into quarters
1/2 cup minced scallions
1 large clove garlic minced

1 cup chopped fresh parsley
2 tablespoons fresh dill
  chopped
1 tablespoon chopped fresh
  mint
3 tablespoons olive oil
juice of 1/2 lemon
1/2 cup chopped roasted
  walnuts
salt and pepper to taste

Bring chicken broth to a boil. Place couscous in another heat-proof bowl and cover with the chicken broth. Using a fork, stir in the olive oil and salt. Cover, set aside for about 5 minutes. Mix the artichoke hearts, scallions, garlic, parsley, dill and mint into the cooked couscous. Stir in the oil, lemon juice and walnuts. Add salt and pepper to taste. Serve at either room temperature or chilled. To roast the walnuts: Place walnuts on ungreased baking sheet and bake at 350° for about 5 minutes, until just lightly browned.

CURRY PILAF

1/4 cup butter or margarine
1 cup chopped onions
1 1/2 cups rice
2 cans consommé

1 cup seedless white raisins
1/2 teaspoon curry powder
salt and pepper to taste

Melt butter in a 2-3 quart flameproof casserole. Stir in onion and rice. Cook over medium heat until golden brown, about 5 minutes, stirring frequently. Add consommè, raisins, curry powder, salt, and pepper and mix well. Cover and cook over low heat for 30 minutes, or until liquid is absorbed.

BLACK BEANS & RICE CASSEROLE

1 15-ounce can black beans, rinsed and drained

1 cup raw rice

2 cups or 1 16-ounce can chicken stock

1 10-ounce box frozen corn kernels

1 13-ounce jar mild salsa (or 8 ounce jar of salsa and 5 ounce can of tomato sauce)

1/2 to 1 cup grated cheddar cheese

Preheat oven to 350°. Mix all ingredients together except cheese. Pour into casserole dish; cover and bake for 1 hour and 15 minutes. Uncover and top with grated cheddar cheese; bake for 10 more minutes. Serve with sour cream and extra salsa. Great one dish meal. Can add cooked chicken breast for non-vegetarians.

MY MOTHER'S BROWN RICE

1 cup extra long grain white rice, uncooked

1 medium onion, chopped

6-12 fresh mushrooms, sliced

1 10 1/2-ounce can consommé

1/2 can water

2 tablespoons butter (more if needed)

Preheat oven to 400°. Sauté rice in butter over medium high heat until rice changes from clear to white (add more butter if rice seems to stop cooking). Add onion; sauté until it turns clear. Transfer to a 2-quart ovensafe dish. Add mushrooms, consommé, water and stir gently to mix well. Cover. Bake 40 minutes or until all liquid is absorbed.

CHARLESTON RED RICE

4 slices bacon

1 cup rice

2 cups tomato juice

1/2 cup onion chopped

1/2 cup chopped green pepper

1/2 teaspoon chili powder

salt and pepper

Fry bacon, add onions and peppers, cook until tender. Add tomato juice, chili powder, salt, pepper and rice. Bring to a boil. Reduce to simmer and cook lightly covered for 30 minutes. Fluff with fork. Crumble bacon on top. Let set for 30 minutes before serving.

Food for thought: There are more than 40,000 varieties of rice; only 20 are produced commercially in the U.S. Americans tend to like rice that cooks up fluffy, with grains that separate.

ROASTED PARMESAN FRENCH FRIES

3 large baking potatoes
1/4 cup butter, melted

1/2 cup grated Parmesan cheese
salt

Cut unpeeled potatoes into long thin strips. Soak in ice water for one hour; drain and plunge into boiling water. Cook for 5 minutes, until almost tender. Drain, rinse in cold water, pat dry. Preheat broiler. Arrange potatoes on cookie sheet. Brush with melted butter; sprinkle with cheese and salt. Broil about 10 minutes until brown and crunchy.

SWISS POTATO SALAD

2 pounds potatoes
2 cups chicken broth
8 teaspoons white wine vinegar
8 teaspoons sunflower oil
1/3 cup Dijon mustard

1/3 cup chopped green onions
1/4 cup chopped baby dill pickles
salt and pepper to taste
2-3 teaspoons finely chopped chives

Wash the potatoes and bring to a boil in salted water. When cooked, drain, and cool.

Peel and slice potatoes and place in large mixing bowl. Warm the chicken broth and stir in 3 teaspoons vinegar, pour over potatoes. Meanwhile, in a medium bowl, blend the remaining vinegar, oil, Dijon mustard, salt and pepper. Next add the green onions and baby dill pickles, mix thoroughly. Pour Dijon mixture over potatoes and mix gently. Let sit at least 1 hour before serving. May be prepared several hours before and chilled. Add the chives just prior to serving.

SMASHED POTATOES WITH ZUCCHINI

4 medium potatoes
   (scrubbed but not peeled)
4 tablespoons butter
1 medium onion, chopped
   fine and sautéed
2 eggs beaten
2 cups grated mozzarella
   cheese

1 cup sour cream
1 large zucchini, grated
1/2 teaspoon salt or garlic salt
1/2 teaspoon fresh ground
   pepper
1 teaspoon rosemary
1 teaspoon paprika
1/3 cup fine bread crumbs

Preheat oven to 375°. Cook potatoes in boiling water until tender. Meanwhile, sauté onions in butter until translucent. When potatoes are tender, drain, peel and mash in a large bowl. Add beaten eggs, sautéed onion, mozzarella, sour cream, grated zucchini and seasonings. Mix well. Pour in greased casserole dish, top with paprika and bread crumbs. Sprinkle with more paprika. Bake for approximately one hour. Note: This may be prepared ahead and refrigerated up to 8 hours before baking. Increase baking time 15-20 minutes. Great for brunch or barbeques.

DOUBLE CHEESE BAKED POTATOES

4 medium potatoes
1 tablespoon margarine
1/2 cup grated smoked cheese
   (cheddar, mozzarella,
   and/or Gouda)

1/2 cup cream cheese with
   chives
1/8 teaspoon pepper
1 to 2 tablespoons milk
2 tablespoons chives

Preheat oven to 425°. Wash potatoes. Rub skin with margarine, prick potatoes with fork. Wrap in foil. Bake for 40-60 minutes and let cool. Cut lengthwise. Place pulp in a bowl. Mix potato pulp, cheeses, pepper, milk and chives. Beat well. Restuff potatoes. Add grated cheese to the top. Bake at 425° for 20 minutes.

Spruce up plain mashed potatoes by adding chopped spinach. Cook and drain a package of frozen chopped spinach. After beating potatoes to desired consistency, fold in spinach. Yummy with sautéed onions and garlic too.

DELMONICO POTATOES

1 large package frozen hash
  browns
$1/2$ pound sharp grated
  cheddar cheese
1 teaspoon dry mustard

$1^1/2$ teaspoons salt
$1/2$ pint whipping cream
1 cup milk
dash pepper
3 dashes nutmeg

Preheat oven to 325°. Thaw potatoes completely. Put in $1^1/2$ quart greased casserole. Heat cream, milk, cheese, mustard, salt, pepper, and nutmeg in a saucepan until cheese melts. Pour over potatoes. DO NOT STIR. Bake for one hour. For a festive look, use O'Brien potatoes.

MAKE-AHEAD MASHED POTATOES

10 large Idaho potatoes,
  peeled and cut in 1" cubes
1 small onion, diced
2 tablespoons butter
$1/4$ cup milk

2 3-ounce packages cream
  cheese, room temperature
$2/3$ cup sour cream
$1/2$ cup grated cheddar cheese
salt, pepper & paprika to taste

Preheat oven to 350°. In 4-quart saucepan, cover potato cubes and onions with salted water. Bring to a boil over medium heat. Simmer until tender and easily pierced with a sharp knife (about 30 minutes). Drain water. Put potatoes in mixing bowl and mash. Add butter, milk, cream cheese, sour cream, salt and pepper. Put in casserole baking dish and top with grated cheese and paprika. Cover and refrigerate for at least $1/2$ hour. Take out of refrigerator $1/2$ hour before baking. Bake uncovered for 30 minutes.

SEAFOOD

SEAFOOD

FROGMORE STEW OR LOW COUNTRY BOIL

skinless sausage,
    cut into 1¹/₂" pieces
corn on the cob,
    broken in half
shrimp (fresh, large, headed)
small new potatoes, cut
    into quarters
4 tablespoons salt

¹/₈ cup pepper
2 stalks celery
1 onion, quartered
1 lemon, quartered
Old Bay Shrimp Seasoning
    (1 bag per 4 pounds of
    shrimp boil)

Frogmore Stew serves 5-100 people. Allow ¹/₂ pound of shrimp, 1 ear of corn, and 6" of sausage per person. Bring water to a boil in a big pot. Add sausage, boil 10 minutes; potatoes, boil 8 minutes; corn boil 5 minutes, shrimp, boil 2-3 minutes. Remove from boiling water, and serve hot with hot melted butter, and seafood sauce (ketchup with lemon juice, Worcestershire, and horseradish). Note: A large pot with colander insert makes it easy to drain.

FOX GRAPE SHRIMP & GRITS

¹/₂ pound shrimp, peeled
    & deveined
2 tablespoons butter
1 tablespoon flour
3 tablespoons chopped onion

¹/₂ cup water
¹/₄ teaspoon thyme
1 bay leaf
¹/₂ teaspoon crushed garlic
1 tablespoon fresh parsley

Brown flour slowly in butter on stove. Add onion and sauté until soft. Add shrimp, stir, and add water and seasonings. Salt and pepper to taste. Simmer until shrimp are pink, 2-3 minutes. Serve over your favorite grits recipe.

St. Helena Island, near Hilton Head, has a small town center called Frogmore. Composed of only a few buildings, the area was reportedly named after an ancestral English country estate. Today this entire area is simply called St. Helena, but old-timers hold dear in their hearts, Frogmore. This "stew" or seafood boil ranks second in popularity only to the Lowcountry Oyster Roast.

HILTON HEAD ISLAND CHEESY SHRIMP & GRITS

FIRST PREPARE BOILED GRITS:

4 cups water
1 cup coarse grits

2 tablespoons butter
1/2 teaspoon salt

In a saucepan bring water to a boil, slowly stir in the grits, reduce heat and stir frequently, cooking 20 minutes Then add butter and salt.

NEXT, CHEESE GRITS:

1 recipe boiled grits
1 cup grated sharp cheddar
1/2 cup grated Parmesan

pinch white pepper
pinch cayenne pepper

To the boiled grits, add the cheeses and peppers.

FINALLY THE SHRIMP:

1 pound fresh shrimp, peeled rinsed and patted dry
6 slices bacon
peanut oil
2 cups sliced mushrooms
1 cup sliced scallions
1 clove garlic, crushed

4 teaspoons lemon juice
Tabasco
chopped parsley
salt and pepper
1 recipe cheese grits (relax, you already made this)

Dice the bacon and cook until browned, but not crisp; drain and set aside. Add small amount of oil to bacon fat in hot skillet. Heat on medium to high until fat is quite hot, then add shrimp. Stir and add mushrooms when the shrimp starts to color, then add remaining ingredients. Divide cheese grits among 4 warm plates. Spoon shrimp over grits and serve immediately. Fantastic!

BARBECUED HOT & SPICY SHRIMP

2 dozen large shrimp,
  washed and headed but
  unpeeled
1/2 cup unsalted butter
  or margarine
1 tablespoon olive oil
1/2 teaspoon salt
1 teaspoon cayenne pepper

1/3 cup Worcestershire sauce
1/2 teaspoon black pepper
1/2 teaspoon thyme
1/2 teaspoon rosemary
1/2 teaspoon oregano
2 garlic cloves, crushed
2 lemons, juice only

Melt butter or margarine in large skillet. Add all ingredients except shrimp and cook over medium heat for about 10 minutes. Add shrimp to pan and cook until shrimp are pink and done throughout, about 10 minutes. Or, place shrimp in oblong baking dish and cover with sauce. Bake at 400° for 15-20 minutes, stirring once or twice. Serve in large dish with juice. Provide French bread for dipping into sauce.

BAKED SHRIMP & ARTICHOKES

2 pounds medium shrimp
  (shell, devein, rinse & drain)
1/3 cup margarine
4-5 cloves garlic, minced
salt
freshly ground pepper

2 6-ounce jars marinated
  artichoke hearts
3 tablespoons lemon juice
1/4 cup dry white wine
parsley chopped
lemon wedges

In a large skillet combine butter and garlic over medium heat until just sizzling. Add shrimp, turning to coat all sides. Sprinkle lightly with salt and pepper. Bake at 400° for 5 minutes – just until shrimp begins to turn pink. Add artichoke hearts with half the marinade, the lemon juice and wine. Return to oven and bake until shrimp are done and artichoke hearts heated through, about 5 minutes longer. Turn into a serving dish. Sprinkle with parsley and serve with lemon wedges.

HOT & CRUSTY SHRIMP

1 pound medium-large shrimp, peeled and deveined, tails on	1/4 -1/2 cup melted butter

SAUCE:

1/2 jar orange marmalade	1-2 teaspoons horseradish

Preheat oven to 350°. Prepare topping; make bread crumbs out of saltines in blender or food processor. Add celery seed, thyme and Parmesan cheese, set aside. In a buttered shallow dish or ramekin, arrange shrimp. Cover with bread crumb mixture. Drizzle with butter. Bake for 15-20 minutes until shrimp are done and topping is brown. While shrimp are cooking, prepare sauce. In a small saucepan, slowly heat marmalade and horseradish; do not boil. Serve shrimp with warm sauce.

SHRIMP NEWBURG

3 pounds shrimp, headed and shelled	3 1/2 tablespoons ketchup
4 1/2 tablespoons flour	1/2 cup sherry
4 1/2 tablespoons butter	1/2 teaspoon salt
2 cups half & half	1/2 teaspoon seasoned salt
2 cups milk	1/4 -1/2 cup melted butter
	pepper to taste

Boil shrimp in salted water for 3 minutes. In a large pan or Dutch oven, combine remaining ingredients. When well mixed and thickened, add shrimp. Simmer on low 5-10 minutes. Serve on rice or pastry shells.

NEW ORLEANS SHRIMP

5 pounds shrimp, cooked and peeled
2 cups celery, finely chopped
1 bunch green onions, finely chopped
1/2 cup olive or salad oil
1/8 cup vinegar

1 tablespoon sugar
1/4 teaspoon Tabasco
1/2 cup chili sauce or catsup
1 tablespoon salt
5 tablespoons horseradish
2 tablespoons prepared mustard

Mix all ingredients except the shrimp together to make the marinade. Cover and refrigerate. Marinate shrimp for a few hours, up to 24 hours. A clove of garlic may be added while marinating. Serve on a bed of lettuce.

SHRIMP CREOLE

1 pound medium shrimp, peeled and deveined
1/4 cup butter
2 bell peppers, sliced
2 onions, sliced
2 stalks celery sliced

1 can whole tomatoes, crushed
2 bay leaves
2 garlic cloves
pinch thyme
salt & pepper to taste

Sauté shrimp in butter for 10 minutes. Add peppers, onions and celery and cook for another 10 minutes. Stir in tomatoes, bay leaves, thyme and garlic. Add salt and pepper and cook for another 10 minutes. Serve over white rice.

BASIL SHRIMP IN FRESH TOMATO SAUCE

3 teaspoons olive oil
1 medium onion, chopped
6 medium cloves garlic, minced
6 large ripe tomatoes, cut into large cubes
6 strips orange peel, no white pith
1 pound large shrimp, peeled, headed and deveined
$1/4$ teaspoon cayenne pepper
$1/2$ cup fresh basil, chopped
$1/2$ pound farfalle (bowtie) pasta
2 tablespoons freshly grated Parmesan cheese

Place a large pot of water on to boil. Meanwhile, in a medium skillet heat the olive oil. Add onions and sauté over medium heat for about 5 minutes. Add garlic and sauté another minute. Add tomatoes and orange peel and cook 15 minutes, stirring occasionally. If the sauce looks watery, raise the heat to high and cook several minutes until thick and reduced. When pot of water comes to a boil, throw in pasta and cook according to directions, drain and set aside.

GO BACK TO THE SHRIMP: Lower heat to medium and add shrimp and cayenne pepper. Allow shrimp to cook approximately 3 minutes or until pink. Add salt and pepper to taste. Remove orange peel and stir in basil. Divide pasta onto 4 plates and spoon shrimp and sauce on top. Sprinkle with Parmesan cheese.

MAY RIVER SHRIMP & CRAB CASSEROLE

1 pound fresh crabmeat
1 pound cooked shrimp, chopped
1 medium green pepper, chopped
1 onion, chopped
1 cup chopped celery
1 cup mayonnaise
1 tablespoon Worcestershire sauce
$1/2$ teaspoon each, salt and pepper
6 saltines crushed
1 tablespoon lemon juice
2 tablespoons sherry
1 cup dry bread crumbs
2 tablespoons melted butter

Mix all ingredients except bread crumbs and melted butter and pour into oblong or oval baking dish. Combine bread crumbs and melted butter and sprinkle on top. Bake uncovered at 350° for 30 minutes.

CRAB SAVANNAH

1 cup crab meat
6 slices toasted bread, crumbled
2 tablespoons butter or margarine, melted
1/2 tablespoon Worcestershire sauce

dash of Tabasco
1/4 teaspoon salt
2 tablespoons light cream
2 tablespoons bread crumbs
1 tablespoon butter or margarine, melted
grated cheese

Mix crab with crumbled toast. Combine butter with Worcestershire sauce, Tabasco, salt and pepper. Mix with crabmeat. Add cream to mixture. Turn into greaséd casserole. Top with bread crumbs mixed with 1 tablespoon of butter. Sprinkle with grated cheese. Bake 30 minutes at 325°.

OKATIE CRAB CASSEROLE

1 cup crabmeat
6 tablespoons margarine
2 tablespoons flour
1 3/4 cups milk
1/2 teaspoon salt
1/2 teaspoon pepper
1 tablespoon Worcestershire sauce

1 teaspoon horseradish
1 teaspoon lemon juice
1/2 teaspoon prepared mustard
2 cups bread crumbs
1/2 cup grated cheddar cheese
1 egg

Preheat oven to 375°. Melt margarine and stir in flour. Add 1 1/2 cups of milk and stir over medium heat until slightly thickened. Add salt, pepper, Worcestershire sauce, horseradish, lemon juice and prepared mustard and mix. Stir in crabmeat and bread crumbs to above mixture. Add grated cheese. If additional moisture is needed, stir in egg beaten with 1/4 cup milk. Sprinkle bread crumbs and grated cheese on top. Bake for about 30 minutes until top is golden brown.

The Lowcountry oyster roast is our most treasured outdoor celebration. Old wooden cable spools serve as tables and an open log fire with a piece of sheet metal suffices as the stove. Mounds of raw oysters collected from the surrounding marshes are piled on the hot fire, covered with burlap, hosed down and steamed slightly open. Friends and family gather around the makeshift tables — most bring their own oyster knife and shucking glove — to devour mounds of the salty local specialty. Cocktail sauce and saltines are the only accompaniment. Cold beer is the drink of choice... And a grand time is had by all!

DAUFUSKIE DEVILED CRAB

1 pound crabmeat
1 cup Ritz cracker crumbs
3 tablespoons onion, chopped
3 tablespoons chopped green pepper
1 stalk celery, chopped

2 tablespoons mayonnaise
1/2 teaspoon dry mustard
1/4 cup ketchup
2-3 eggs beaten
Tabasco
salt and pepper

Sauté onion, pepper, celery in butter for 1-2 minutes. Remove from heat. Add mayonnaise, mustard, ketchup, eggs, Tabasco, salt and pepper and one half of cracker crumbs. Mix well with fork. Pack in clean crab shells, top with remaining cracker crumbs. Bake for 30 minutes at 350°.

SCALLOPS WITH ASPARAGUS

2 pounds thin asparagus, rinsed
1 pound bay or sea scallops

1 medium sweet onion, chopped
2 tablespoons canola oil

DRESSING:
2/3 cup olive oil
1/3 cup herb vinegar
1/4 cup virgin peanut oil
salt

freshly ground black pepper
1 tablespoon chopped fresh parsley

Snap off the thick wood ends of the asparagus. Peel the stalk with a vegetable peeler, beginning at the little offshoots near the tips. Place in a large pot or frying pan with enough boiling water to cover. Cook, uncovered, briefly until just done and still crisp, about 3-5 minutes. Rinse in cold water and set aside.

Make the dressing by combining the olive oil with the vinegar, using a wire whisk. Taste and add peanut oil as desired for flavor. Season with salt, pepper and parsley. Toss the still-warm asparagus in some of the dressing. Set aside. Refrigerate only if necessary! The asparagus will change color when refrigerated. Set the remaining dressing aside. In a skillet, heat the 2 tablespoons canola oil in a large saucepan, add the onion and cook until soft. Add the scallops and cook for 5 minutes. Remove and toss warm scallops in remaining dressing. Chill. When ready to serve, place some of the asparagus on each plate, and top with the scallops and dressing.

Daufuskie deviled crabs are a closely guarded secret recipe of the natives of neighboring Daufuskie Island. The ladies sit out by Daufuskie's public dock, and peddle their own private version of deviled crabs from large aluminum foil-covered metal bowls to passing boaters and tourists. For an island accessible only by water, these cooks do a fine business.

RED SNAPPER
IN CREAMY COCONUT SAUCE

2 pounds white fish
   (red snapper or tilapia)
6 garlic cloves, crushed
1 tablespoon ginger, crushed
1 large lime, juice only
pinch of salt

pinch of ground pepper
2 tablespoons vegetable oil
1/2 purple onion
1/2 tomato
2 1/2 -3 cups thick coconut
   milk

Marinate the fish in the garlic, ginger, lime juice, salt and pepper for at least one hour. Fry the fish lightly in the oil, then remove and set aside. In a blender puree the onion and tomato, add 1/2 cup of the coconut milk and mix. Return fish to a clean pan, add tomato mixture and simmer gently. Add more coconut milk to taste, at least 2 cups. Simmer gently for 20 minutes. The sauce should be light, not thick. Serve over rice.

TANGERINE TUNA

4 tuna steaks, cut 1/4-1/2" thick

MARINADE:

1/4 cup soy sauce
1/4 cup fresh tangerine juice (or substitute orange juice)
4 strips (1/2" each) tangerine zest (or orange)
3 tablespoons honey
2 tablespoons Oriental sesame oil
3 cloves garlic, minced

2 scallions, trimmed and minced, reserve green part for garnish
1 tablespoon minced fresh ginger
3 strips lemon zest (1 1/2" long)
1 tablespoon Oriental sesame oil for brushing tuna
2 tablespoons toasted sesame seeds

Toasting seeds: Place seeds in dry skillet over medium heat. Cook 1- 2 minutes, shaking pan until seeds are aromatic (white seeds should turn light brown).

Preheat barbecue grill to very hot. Rinse fish steaks and pat dry. In a shallow bowl, whisk together all ingredients for marinade. Place tuna in non-reactive baking dish, pour marinade over tuna. Marinate covered in refrigerator for 30-60 minutes, turning once. Drain tuna steaks and blot dry. Brush with sesame oil. Grill tuna one minute per side or until cooked to taste. Sprinkle with chopped scallion greens and sesame seeds.

PESTO SWORDFISH KABOBS

1 clove garlic
1 cup packed fresh basil leaves
2 tablespoons extra virgin olive oil
1 tablespoon red wine vinegar

1 pound - 3/4" thick swordfish steaks, skinned and cut into 1" cubes
1/8 teaspoon pepper
vegetable cooking spray

Position knife blade in food processor bowl, top with cover. With processor running, drop garlic through food chute; process until finely chopped. With processor running, add basil through food chute; process until finely chopped. Scrape basil mixture into a small bowl, using a rubber spatula. Add olive oil and vinegar; stir well and set aside. Sprinkle fish with pepper; thread onto 4 (12") skewers. Coat grill rack with vegetable cooking spray; place on grill over medium-hot coals. Place swordfish kabobs on grill rack, and cook 4 minutes on each side or until fish flakes easily when tested with a fork, basting frequently with basil mixture.

ATLANTIC FILLETS WITH SAFFRON & GARLIC

1 pound fresh fish fillets
pinch of saffron threads
1 tablespoon boiling water
2 tablespoons butter
3 cloves of garlic, minced

1 tablespoon fresh lemon
   juice
1/4 teaspoon ground fennel
1 tomato diced
salt and pepper to taste

Rinse the fish and set aside. Into a small bowl, crumble the saffron, add the boiling water and set aside. In a saucepan, melt the butter, add the garlic and sauté until soft. Stir in the lemon juice, fennel, tomatoes and saffron liquid. Add the fish fillets, spoon the sauce over the fish and sprinkle with salt and pepper. Cover the saucepan and cook on low heat for 10 minutes, or until the fish flakes easily with a fork. Serve immediately.

CAJUN GROUPER FILLET

1 1/2 pounds grouper fillet
Tony Chachere's Cajun
   Seasoning (to taste,
   a little goes a long way)

1-2 tablespoons butter
Parmesan cheese

Preheat oven to 450°. Place grouper in a greased baking dish, sprinkle on seasoning and Parmesan cheese, dot with butter, and bake for approximately 20 minutes until fish is flaky.

COCONUT CRUSTED SOLE

**2 pounds fillet of sole, fresh
    or frozen
2 cups fine cracker crumbs
1 cup flaked coconut
2 eggs, beaten**

**2 tablespoons evaporated
    milk
$1/2$ teaspoon salt
$1/2$ cup cooking oil**

Thaw fillets if necessary. In a large shallow bowl combine
cracker crumbs and coconut. In a small bowl combine eggs,
milk and salt. Dip fish in egg mixture, then drag through
cracker coconut mixture. Heat 2-3 tablespoons oil in skillet.
Arrange fillets in single layer. Fry over moderate heat for 5-8
minutes, until brown. Garnish with fruit and serve.

HINTS FOR COOKING FISH

LEAN, MILD, FIRM FLESH

Halibut
Flounder
Grouper
Red Snapper

Best when broiled,
sautéed, poached
or baked

FATTER FISH

Swordfish
Salmon
Mackerel
Mahi-Mahi

Best when grilled,
poached, broiled,
or baked

PAN-SIZED WHOLE FISH

Mackerel
Smelt
Trout

Best when butter sautéed,
fried, oven-fried, broiled or
grilled

CHICKEN

CHICKEN

CHICKEN WITH CRANBERRY & PEARS

4 whole chicken breasts,
  skinned boned halved
  and floured
1/2 cup butter
2 large garlic cloves, minced
2 tablespoons shallots,
  minced
4 tablespoons flour

1 cup fresh cranberries,
  coarsely chopped
4 ripe pears, peeled and
  sliced
1 cup heavy cream
1 cup sour cream
1/4 cup chopped fresh parsley

*Chicken combines
beautifully with
every imaginable
flavor...
including
cranberry
and pears.*

Melt half the butter in a large heavy skillet. Add garlic and
shallot, cook one minute. Lightly flour chicken breasts and
cook until done. Remove to platter and keep warm. Add
cranberries to pan; cook and stir for one minute. Add pears
and cook until slightly softened. Add creams, stir and heat
through, but don't boil. Pour sauce over chicken and sprinkle
with fresh parsley. Can be made ahead and rewarmed in a
covered dish at low temperature in oven.

CHICKEN BY THE SEA

4 chicken breasts, boiled and
  cut into bite sized pieces
3/4 package sea shell pasta,
  cooked and drained
1 can cream of chicken soup
1 can cream of celery soup
1 cup chicken stock or broth
1/2 lemon, juice only

1 tablespoon mayonnaise
8 ounces sour cream
2-3 tablespoons butter
2 cups grated mozzarella
  cheese
Italian bread crumbs
chicken broth

Preheat oven to 350°. Cook noodles in extra chicken broth, or
water, undercook slightly. Mix soups, sour cream, chicken
broth, lemon juice, mayonnaise and sour cream. Toss sea
shells with 1 1/2 tablespoons butter and stir in soup mixture. In
a greased casserole dish, layer 1/3 of pasta, chicken and
mozzarella. Repeat layers and dot with remaining butter.
Top with Italian bread crumbs and bake uncovered approximately 40 minutes. This freezes very well; make sure to cover
tightly and increase baking time by about 10 minutes if
you've had it in the freezer.

LEMON CHICKEN WITH BROWN SUGAR CRUST

2 chickens, cut into quarters   **2 cups fresh lemon juice**

Combine chicken pieces and lemon juice in a bowl. Cover and marinate in the refrigerator overnight, turning occasionally.

The key to this recipe is marinating the chicken in the lemon juice overnight.

2 cups flour
2 teaspoons salt
2 teaspoons paprika
1 teaspoon freshly ground black pepper
1/2 cup corn oil

2 tablespoons grated lemon zest
1/4 cup brown sugar
1/4 cup chicken stock
1 teaspoon lemon extract
2 lemons, sliced paper thin

Preheat oven to 350°. Drain chicken thoroughly and pat dry. Fill a plastic bag with flour, salt, paprika and pepper. Put two pieces of chicken into the bag at a time and shake, coating completely. Heat corn oil in frying pan until hot and fry chicken a few pieces at a time, until well browned and crisp. Arrange chicken in a single layer in a large shallow baking pan. Sprinkle evenly with brown sugar and top with lemon zest. Mix chicken stock and lemon extract together, pour around chicken pieces. Set a thin lemon slice on top of each piece of chicken. Bake 35-40 minutes. Serve with mashed potatoes and carrots.

AWESOME ASPARAGUS CHICKEN

4 chicken breasts, stewed and torn into bite sized pieces
1 bunch (2 pounds) fresh asparagus, steamed
1 can cream of chicken soup

1 can cream of mushroom soup
1 1/2 cups milk
2 eggs boiled
2 cups grated or diced cheddar cheese

Preheat oven to 350°. In greased casserole dish, layer drained asparagus and chicken. In a medium saucepan mix soups and milk over low flame until smooth. Ladle 1/3 of soup mixture over asparagus and chicken. Top with thinly sliced boiled eggs and cheddar cheese. Pour remaining soup mixture over all and bake about 50 minutes.

CRANBERRY ISLAND CHICKEN BREASTS

10 boneless chicken breasts, halved
1 can whole berry cranberry sauce

1 8-ounce jar Catalina or French dressing
1 package Lipton onion soup mix

Preheat oven to 350°. Mix together the cranberry sauce, dressing and soup mix. Spray non-stick cooking spray in 9 x 13" glass casserole, add chicken breasts, top with cranberry mixture. Bake uncovered for 45-50 minutes.

MARGARITA GRILLED CHICKEN

6 boneless chicken breasts

MARINADE:
$2/3$ cup olive oil
$1/2$ cup lime juice
$1/4$ cup Tequila

2 tablespoons Triple Sec
$1/4$ cup minced fresh cilantro

Mix all marinade ingredients together in a shallow non-metallic pan. Add chicken and coat with marinade. Cover and refrigerate for 4 hours. Remove from refrigerator 30 minutes before cooking. Preheat outdoor grill. Grill chicken on both sides, basting frequently until chicken is cooked throughout. Serve with salsa.

CANTON CHICKEN

$2^1/_2$-3 pound broiler-fryer, cut up
10 ounce jar apricot preserves or orange marmalade

$1/4$ cup soy sauce
$1/4$ cup sherry
$1/4$ cup onion, finely chopped

Preheat oven to 325°. Place chicken in $11^3/_4$ x $7^1/_2$" baking dish. Combine ingredients; pour over chicken. Bake for one hour turning occasionally. Serve with rice and a tossed salad of mixed greens.

Keep apricot preserves or orange marmalade on hand for this quick to prepare and satisfying dinner.

CITRUS CHICKEN

4-6 skinless chicken breasts   **2 stalks celery, chopped**
lemon pepper   **parsley**
³/₄ cup orange juice

For a richer dish,
toss in
1 tablespoon
. of sour cream
or cream cheese
to pasta.

Brown chicken 2-3 minutes each side with oil and lemon pepper to season. Then pour ¹/₂ of orange juice over chicken, cover and simmer on medium-low heat about 10 minutes. Turn chicken, adding chopped celery and remainder of orange juice. Simmer on medium-low heat another 10 minutes. Serve over pasta with mandarin oranges.

CHICKEN DIVINE

4 chicken breasts, cooked   **¹/₄ cup lemon juice**
** & chopped**   **1 cup grated cheddar cheese**
2 10-ounce packages frozen   **1 cup bread crumbs**
** broccoli spears**   **1 teaspoon curry, or to taste**
2 cans cream of chicken soup   **1 teaspoon paprika**
1 cup mayonnaise

This is a great
"make ahead of
time, keep in the
refrigerator and
throw in the oven
when ready"
dinner!

Preheat oven to 350°. Boil broccoli slightly, then chop and put in bottom of buttered casserole. Layer chicken over broccoli. Mix a sauce of the soup, mayonnaise, lemon juice and curry and cover the chicken with it. Top with grated cheese and sprinkle with bread crumbs and paprika. Bake 35-40 minutes.

INCREDIBLE CHICKEN

chicken pieces, boneless or
with bones

brown sugar
garlic salt

Preheat oven to 375°. Clean chicken pieces. Sprinkle generous amount of brown sugar on chicken, shake garlic salt on top. Bake for 45 minutes or until brown; for boneless breasts reduce cooking time to 30 minutes. Good served hot or cold.

LARRY'S GRILLED CHICKEN

chicken breasts

T. Marzetti's spinach salad
dressing

Marinate skinless, boneless chicken breasts in T. Marzetti's spinach salad dressing for several hours. Cook on grill, basting with marinade. Top with grilled onions and green peppers.

LAUREN'S LEMON CHICKEN

8 chicken breasts

MARINADE:
1 cup extra virgin olive oil
1 cup lemon juice
1 tablespoon soy sauce
1 tablespoon Worcestershire
1 tablespoon red wine
vinegar

1 tablespoon Teriyaki
1 tablespoon honey
1-3 tablespoons Mrs. Dash
lemon & herb seasoning

Clean and dry chicken. Mix together marinade ingredients, add cleaned chicken pieces. Marinate for 3-6 hours. Grill or broil both sides. Do not marinate longer than 6 hours or chicken will be dry when cooked.

Food for thought: Always cook chicken until it is well done. Never thaw chicken on the counter or at room temperature, defrost chicken in the refrigerator or microwave.

Grill extra breasts of lemon chicken for a great salad the next day... Cut up chicken pieces toss with romaine lettuce, crumbled blue cheese, raisins, green onions and avocados and your favorite vinegar based Italian dressing.

HONEY CURRY CHICKEN

3 pounds, chicken cut into
  pieces
4 tablespoons butter
1/2 cup honey

1/4 cup Dijon mustard
1 teaspoon salt
1 teaspoon curry powder
  or to taste

Preheat oven to 375°. Wash, dry and skin chicken. Melt butter and add remaining ingredients. Dip chicken pieces in honey mixture to coat both sides. Arrange chicken in casserole, meaty side up in single layer. Pour extra sauce on chicken. Bake uncovered for 45 minutes-1 hour (depending on the thickness of pieces), or until chicken is tender and glazed. Basting during cooking gives a more even glaze. Serve with rice pilaf and green salad with Mandarin oranges.

CHICKEN TETRAZZINI

1 chicken or 4 breasts,
  cooked & diced
1/4 cup green chiles
1/4 cup scallions
4 ounces chopped
  mushrooms
3 tablespoons butter
1 cup chicken broth

1 cup half & half
1 small jar pimentos drained
2 tablespoons sherry
1/2 cup Parmesan cheese
6 ounces spaghetti noodles
  cooked
salt and pepper to taste

Preheat oven to 300°. Sauté chiles, scallions and mushrooms in 3 tablespoons butter, approximately 5 minutes. In separate pan, warm chicken broth and half & half. Add 3 tablespoons flour. When this becomes thickened, add pimentos, sherry and Parmesan cheese. Add sautéed vegetables along with salt and pepper. Add diced chicken and spaghetti noodles. Bake 20-30 minutes.

CHICKEN DIJON

2 4-ounce chicken breasts,
  pounded flat
1/2 cup chicken broth
1 tablespoon Dijon mustard
1 1/2 garlic cloves, minced
freshly ground black pepper
2 tablespoons flour
1/2 teaspoon salt
1/2 teaspoon white pepper

1/2 teaspoon black pepper
1/2 teaspoon thyme
1 tablespoon canola oil
2 green onions, chopped
5-7 spears of asparagus
1-1 1/2 ounces grated fresh
  mozzarella
2 tablespoons Parmesan
  cheese

Mix together the chicken broth, Dijon and garlic and then the ground pepper to taste and set aside. Mix together the flour, salt and peppers, and thyme. Dredge the chicken in flour mixture. Sauté chicken in the canola oil until lightly browned. Turn chicken over and pour in broth mixture. Add onions. Top with asparagus and then cheese. Heat to melt. Serve with side of rice or pasta.

POPPY SEED CHICKEN CASSEROLE

8 chicken breasts
2 cups sour cream
2 cans cream of chicken soup
1 cup chicken broth

2 tablespoons poppy seeds
1 8-ounce box Ritz crackers
3/4 cup butter

Prepare this ahead
of time and
refrigerate until
ready to bake.

Preheat oven to 350°. Boil chicken until done; debone. Mix sour cream, soup, chicken broth and poppy seeds and chicken. Crush crackers and mix with melted butter. Place layer of chicken, layer of crackers, layer of chicken, and end with cracker layer. Bake for one hour.

CHICKEN & ALMOND CASSEROLE

3 cups cooked diced chicken
1 can cream of mushroom
   soup
1 cup chopped celery
1 cup sliced mushrooms

2 teaspoons grated white
   onion or scallions
2 cups cooked rice
1 teaspoon lemon juice
1 small can sliced water
   chestnuts

TOPPING:
1 cup corn flakes, crushed $^1/_4$ cup melted butter
$^1/_2$ cup slivered almonds

Preheat oven to 350°. Toss all ingredients except those for topping in large bowl. Place in a 9 x 13" buttered casserole. Bake for 20 minutes. Meanwhile, in a small bowl, combine ingredients for topping. Spread the topping evenly over chicken mixture. Bake another 20 minutes, until bubbly.

CHICKEN & STUFFING WITH LEMON HONEY GLAZE

4 chicken breast halves
1 14$^1/_2$-ounce can vegetable
   broth
2 tablespoons margarine
2 medium carrots
5 cups herb seasoned stuffing

2 tablespoons honey
2 tablespoons lemon juice
1 tablespoon chopped fresh
   parsley or 1 teaspoon
   dried parsley flakes

Preheat oven to 375°. In a saucepan combine broth, margarine, and carrots. Heat to boiling and remove from heat. Add stuffing, toss to mix well. Spoon into a greased oblong baking dish. Arrange chicken (bone side down on stuffing mixture). In a small bowl, combine honey, lemon juice, and parsley. Brush on chicken. Bake for one hour or until chicken is no longer pink and juices run clear. Stir stuffing before serving.

"The young child passes through a series of sensitive periods during which he experiences an intense and specialized interest in the things around him."
— Maria Montessori

SMOTHERED CHICKEN

6 chicken breasts, skinless
6 slices Swiss cheese
1 can cream of mushroom soup

1 package dry stuffing
¼ cup margarine melted

Preheat oven to 350°. Place chicken breasts in a shallow baking dish. Place a slice of Swiss cheese on each chicken breast. Top with cream of mushroom soup. Sprinkle stuffing over top and evenly pour melted margarine over all. Bake for 40 minutes.

CHICKEN SQUARES

8 large chicken breasts
1 cup sour cream
1 can cream of mushroom soup
1 cup sliced mushrooms

1 cup mayonnaise
2 packages Pillsbury crescent rolls
1-2 tablespoons butter
Parmesan cheese

Preheat oven to 400°. Brown chicken thoroughly and separate into small pieces. In a separate bowl combine with sour cream, soup, mushrooms and mayonnaise. Season to taste. Roll out crescent rolls so seams are together to form square. Spread them with butter and sprinkle with Parmesan cheese. Add chicken mixture. Fold corner to corner to cover. Bake for 20 minutes or until golden.

QUICK-N-DELICIOUS CHICKEN PIE

5 boned chicken breasts
3 stalks celery, chopped
4 carrots, diced
1 small onion, finely chopped
1 teaspoon poultry seasoning

salt and pepper to taste
1 package ready made pie
crust (found in your
grocer's dairy section)
3 heaping tablespoons flour

Preheat oven to 400°. Cook chicken breasts and next 5 ingredients, in water to cover for one hour or until tender. Strain the broth and save for use with flour for gravy. Break the chicken in small pieces and put chicken, celery, carrots and onion in bottom of pie crust. Mix broth with flour to make gravy. Pour enough gravy over chicken to cover. Put top of crust on and flute the edges. Bake at 400° for approximately 20 minutes or until brown.Great served with rice, black-eyed peas and tomato salsa.

EASY CHICKEN POT PIE

4 cups cubed cooked chicken
1 10-ounce package frozen
mixed vegetables, thawed
and drained
2 cans condensed cream of
chicken soup

1$\frac{1}{2}$ cups chicken broth
2 cups Bisquick
$\frac{1}{2}$ tablespoon thyme
$\frac{1}{4}$ teaspoon sage
1$\frac{1}{2}$ cups milk

Preheat oven to 350°. Spread chicken and vegetables in ungreased 13 x 9 x 2" pan. Mix soup and chicken broth. Pour into pan. Mix remaining ingredients. Pour evenly over soup mixture. (Crust will rise during baking.) Bake for 50-60 minutes or until golden brown.

Chicken pies have been popular since the Colonial times. Some chicken pies were made with whole birds baked in a pot covered with pastry, while others used chopped vegetables and poultry coated in gravy and baked with a pastry covering. Here are two of the latter variations to add to your repertoire.

CHILI CHICKEN CASSEROLE

4 ounces tortilla chips
1 pound boneless chicken breasts, cubed
1 small onion, diced
1 clove garlic, minced
2 tablespoons oil
1 15-ounce can tomato sauce
1 15½-ounce can dark red kidney beans, drained
½ cup each sliced black and green olives

3 tablespoons chili powder
½ teaspoon crushed red pepper flakes
1 teaspoon black pepper
1 tablespoon basil
1 tablespoon parsley
1 cup grated Monterey Jack
1 cup grated cheddar cheese

On a chilly winter evening delight your family with a hearty one-dish dinner.

Preheat oven to 350°. Line bottom of 13 x 9 x 2" pan with chips. In a large pan, on the stovetop, sauté chicken, onions and garlic in oil over medium heat. Stir in all remaining ingredients except cheese, cover and cook 35 minutes. Pour chicken mixture over chips. Top with cheese. Bake in oven briefly until cheese melts, 5 -7 minutes.

MEXICAN CHICKEN & RICE

1 pound chicken breast halves, skinless, boneless
1 tablespoon cooking oil
½ cup chopped onion
1 clove garlic minced
1 can Ro★tel tomatoes
1 can low sodium chicken broth

1¾ cup quick-cooking brown rice
dash or two Tabasco
1 cup grated Monterey Jack cheese
sliced olives (optional)
sour cream (optional)

Fresh cooked corn cut off the cob adds a tasty dimension to this dish.

Preheat oven to 350°. In a large skillet cook chicken in hot oil about 2 minutes on each side or until brown; remove and set aside. In same small skillet cook onion, pepper and garlic until tender but not brown. Drain off fat. Stir in undrained tomatoes, broth, uncooked rice and Tabasco. Cut cooled chicken into smaller pieces and add to mixture. Bring to boil; remove from heat and spoon mixture into a 12 x 8 x 2" baking dish. Bake covered, for 30 minutes. Pile on the Jack cheese. Place under broiler for a few minutes until cheese is brown and bubbly. Enjoy with olives and sour cream. Guacamole is great with this!

CHINESE CHICKEN CASSEROLE

3 chicken breasts, cooked
  and diced
1 can celery soup
1 can Chinese vegetables
1 can French style green
  beans

1 package curried rice
1 can water chestnuts,
  chopped
1 cup mayonnaise
$1/2$ cup chicken stock

Preheat oven to 300°. Prepare curried rice as directed on package. Meanwhile in a large mixing bowl, combine all ingredients, then stir in rice. Put chicken mixture in greased casserole dish. Bake for one hour, until bubbly.

HOT CHICKEN SANDWICH MIX

2 boneless chicken breasts,
  cooked and cubed

1 can cream of chicken soup
1 cup crushed potato chips

Microwave for 10 minutes or heat in crock pot. Serve on buns.

BEEF & PORK

BEEF & PORK

FLANK STEAK

1 pound flank steak
1 teaspoon salt
1/2 teaspoon pepper
1/2 teaspoon basil
1/2 teaspoon rosemary

1 clove garlic, crushed
1/2 medium onion, chopped
1 tablespoons wine vinegar
4 tablespoons salad oil

Combine seasonings with oil and vinegar. Brush both sides of steak. Let stand covered in refrigerator overnight. Broil steak on both sides until desired doneness. Slice thin on the diagonal. Spoon pan juices over meat to serve.

ICED BEEF TENDERLOIN

1 pound trimmed center cut
  tenderloin
1 pound rock salt
thyme

tarragon
bay leaf chopped
cracked white pepper

Aïoli - a strongly flavored garlic mayonnaise from the Provence region of southern France

Roll the tenderloin in the herbs and place in a paté dish and cover with rock salt all around. Let stand at room temperature for 4 hours. Shake off salt and roll in foil and put in freezer until frozen. Slice paper thin and serve on ice cold plates. Garnish with a salad and with sour cream and aïoli.

GRILLED BEEF TENDERLOIN

1 5-pound tenderloin
1/4 teaspoon garlic salt
1/4 teaspoon celery salt

1/4 teaspoon onion salt
1 lemon (juice only)

Combine salts with lemon juice. Rub this mixture into meat. Allow to sit in covered glass dish in refrigerator overnight. Grill meat over hot coals about 30 minutes, or until thickest portion reaches 140°. This will provide you with some rare meat, some medium rare and some less rare meat on the ends. Allow to stand about 10 minutes before cutting.

VEAL STEW WITH ROQUEFORT

1 1/2 pound veal cut in cubes	4 medium potatoes, sliced
3-5 tablespoons flour	4 carrots, sliced
1 tablespoon butter	2 onions, sliced
1 tablespoon olive oil	1/4 cup chopped parsley
1 1/2 teaspoon salt	1/4 cup crumbled Roquefort
1/4 teaspoon pepper	cheese
1 1/2 quarts hot water	1/2 cup dry white wine

Coat the veal in flour. Brown veal in butter and oil in a Dutch oven or heavy frying pan. Add salt, pepper and water and simmer for one hour until tender. Add the potatoes, carrots, onions and parsley. Cook 1/2 hour more, until vegetables are tender. Remove meat and vegetables to hot platter. Add the cheese and wine to the remaining sauce. Cook until cheese is melted. Pour sauce over meat and vegetables.

5-HOUR GOLFER'S POT ROAST

1 London broil	ground black pepper
dash of Worcestershire	3-4 bay leaves
1 can tomato soup	4-6 baking potatoes, peeled
2 tablespoons Minute tapioca	4-6 celery stalks
1 teaspoon yellow mustard	2-3 whole onions, peeled
celery salt	6-8 whole carrots grated

Preheat oven to 250°. Mix Worcestershire, soup, tapioca, mustard and seasonings in bottom of air-tight roasting pan. Lay the vegetables in bottom of pan over sauce mixture. Put London broil on top of vegetables. Salt and pepper each layer. Put on tight lid and bake for 5 hours.

FOOL PROOF POT ROAST

1 boneless Chuck Roast   **1 jar white horseradish**
1-3 onions, sliced
1 can whole berry cranberry
  sauce

In a Dutch oven sauté onions until soft. Sear sides of roast by browning sides in Dutch oven with onions. Add cranberry sauce and horseradish. Cover and cook until tender. Test for tenderness after 2½ hours. Depending on size of meat, can cook up to 4 hours. Both cranberry and horseradish join to mellow flavors–great gravy.

EASY DAY POT ROAST

1 lean boneless chuck roast,   **¼ cup light brown sugar,**
  about 3 pounds   **finely packed**
1 28-ounce can of tomatoes   **1 apple, cored and thinly**
1 16-ounce can sauerkraut   **sliced**
                          1 envelope onion gravy mix

Remove visible fat from roast. Place in Dutch oven. Add tomatoes, sauerkraut, brown sugar and apple. Cover and simmer 2½ to 3 hours, until meat is very tender. Remove for heat, skim off excess fat. Stir in gravy mix; heat to boiling, stirring until gravy thickens. Add a little more water if gravy is too thick. Serve with rice.

Note: Can be baked in oven, covered, at 350° for 2½-3 hours if desired.

This recipe created quite a stir scratched on a torn piece of paper with just 4 ingredients. We all were intrigued, and several of us made it for our families... it was unanimously adored! The melding of the flavors is mouthwatering.

BABY POT ROASTS

flank steak	1 can peas and juice
1/4 cup brown mustard	1/4 teaspoon salt
6-8 carrots	1/4 teaspoon pepper

Drain peas over a small bowl, set peas aside. Measure out 1/4 cup of the pea liquid and set the rest aside. Pound the flank steak until about 1/4" thick. Cut into 1 1/2" strips across the grain. Spread generously with mustard, salt and pepper. Chop carrots into 2" lengths. Wrap strip around carrot, (may need more than 1 carrot). Secure with toothpick or string (preferable). In a skillet sear the meat. Add 1/4 cup of pea juice, cover and simmer 2 to 3 hours. Mix remaining pea juice with 3/4 cup catsup. Add to skillet when 1/2 hour remains in cooking time.

STROGANOFF SUPERB

1 pound round steak, cut into thin strips	1/4 teaspoon dry mustard
3 tablespoons margarine	1/4 teaspoon pepper
1/2 cup chopped onion	8 ounces cream cheese, cubed
4 ounce can mushrooms, drained	3/4 cup milk
1/2 teaspoon salt	

In a large frying pan or Dutch oven, brown meat in margarine. Add onion, mushrooms and seasonings; cook 5 minutes or until tender. Add cream cheese and milk; stir over low heat until smooth. Serve over noodles tossed with parsley.

ENCHILADA CASSEROLE

1 tablespoon corn oil
2 pounds ground beef
1 cup chopped onion
1 cup chopped sweet green
  pepper
2 cloves garlic, finely
  chopped
1 cup fresh or frozen whole
  kernel corn
1 16-ounce can stewed
  tomatoes

1 15-ounce can tomato sauce
1 4-ounce can chopped mild
  green chilies
1 teaspoon chili powder
1 teaspoon ground cumin
16 corn tortillas
1 pound Monterey Jack or
  white cheddar cheese, grated
1 8-ounce jar prepared salsa
2 tablespoons chopped green
  onion

Preheat oven to 400°. In a large skillet, heat oil over high heat. Add beef, onion, pepper, and garlic. Sauté, stirring constantly, until meat is browned and onion is tender-about 10 minutes. Drain off fat. Stir in corn and remove mixture to large bowl. In same skillet, heat stewed tomatoes, tomato sauce, chilies, chili powder, and cumin to boiling, stirring to break up pieces of tomato. Spoon 1/2 cup of sauce into bottom of shallow 3 quart oval baking pan or 13 x 9" baking dish. Stir 1/2 cup sauce into meat mixture.

Working on waxed paper, dip a tortilla in sauce, then fill with 1/4 cup meat mixture and 2 tablespoons cheese. Roll up and place in baking pan. Repeat to make 2 layers of 8 enchiladas. Stir any remaining meat mixture into sauce. Pour over enchiladas. Sprinkle with remaining cheese. Spoon salsa over top. Bake 25-30 minutes, or until bubbly and golden brown. Sprinkle with chopped green onion. Serve immediately, or if desired keep warm in the oven until ready to serve.

After a day at the beach, invite your neighbors for dinner. Serve with a salad, have your neighbor bring dessert.

CLASSIC MEATLOAF

3 slices white bread, torn into
  small pieces
1/4 cup skim milk
1 1/4 pounds lean ground beef
2 large eggs, slightly beaten
1 garlic clove, minced

1/4 cup chopped onion
1/2 teaspoon salt
1/4 teaspoon dry mustard
1/4 teaspoon fresh ground
  pepper
1/4 cup ketchup

Preheat oven to 350°. Soak bread in milk for 5 minutes. Add to this remaining ingredients. Shape into loaf and put in loaf pan. Bake 50-60 minutes.

ONION ZEST MEATLOAF

2 1/2-3 pounds ground beef
1 large carrot, grated
1 medium onion, diced
1 package Lipton onion soup
  mix

1 egg
1 cup corn flakes
1/2 teaspoon garlic powder

TOPPING:
1/2 cup ketchup
1 tablespoon bold and spicy
  mustard

2 tablespoons brown sugar

Preheat oven to 350°. Mix the first 7 ingredients together and place in a 9 x 13" pan. Add topping and bake for 60 minutes.

SCALLOPED POTATOES WITH HAM & BROCCOLI

6 baking potatoes	2 cups milk
4 large Vidalia onions	1/4 cup flour
2 cups grated sharp cheddar cheese	2 teaspoons salt
2 cups diced ham	1/2 teaspoon paprika
1 cup cooked and diced broccoli (tops and all)	1 teaspoon pepper

Preheat oven to 325°. Thinly slice the potatoes and onions. Grease a 9 x 13" casserole or similar size. Place a layer of potatoes followed by the onions then broccoli, ham and cheese, repeat layers in same order 1-2 times. In a medium saucepan on low to medium heat, warm the milk, while stirring constantly, add the flour, salt, paprika and pepper. Heat until thickened, turn up the heat if necessary. Pour the cream sauce over the casserole. Bake for one hour, until bubbly.

Food for thought: Use leftover holiday ham for this one dish meal.

BROWN SUGAR PORK TENDERLOIN WITH MUSTARD SAUCE

2 1-1 1/2-pound pork tenderloins	1/4 cup bourbon
1/4 cup soy sauce	2 tablespoons brown sugar

Preheat oven to 325°. Combine all ingredients except for the tenderloins in baking dish; add tenderloins. Cover and refrigerate at least 2 hours, turning occasionally. Remove from marinade and place on rack in roasting pan and bake for 45 minutes or 160° internal temperature. Or grill on medium coals. Serve with mustard sauce.

MUSTARD SAUCE:

2/3 cup sour cream	3-4 green onions finely chopped
2/3 cup mayonnaise	
2 tablespoons dry mustard	

Combine all ingredients; cover and chill until ready to serve.

WINE BRAISED PORK TENDERLOIN

2 pork tenderloins	2 cups chicken stock
1 tablespoon olive oil	2 tablespoons tomato paste
2 tablespoons butter	$1/2$ teaspoon oregano
1 onion, chopped	1 tablespoon cornstarch
1 clove garlic, minced	3 tablespoons cold water
1 pound mushrooms, halved	salt & pepper
$1/2$ cup dry white wine	

Preheat oven to 350°. Heat oil and butter in large oven proof sauté pan over medium heat. When hot, add pork and sear 10-12 minutes on all sides, seasoning while cooking. Remove pork and set aside. Add onion and garlic to pan, cook 3 minutes. Add mushrooms, increase heat to high, cook 5 minutes. Pour in wine and cook 3 minutes. Add chicken stock, tomato paste and oregano. Mix well. Return pork to pan, cover and cook 25 minutes in oven. Remove pork, slice $1/2$" thick set aside. Dissolve cornstarch in water, and stir into sauce until well incorporated. Season and cook a minute. Return meat to sauce, simmer 2 minutes over low heat. Serve with noodles or mashed potatoes.

PORK CHOPS DIVAN

4 large loin pork chops	$1/3$ cup dry white wine
2 tablespoons vegetable oil	$1/3$ cup heavy cream
1 tablespoon butter	2 tablespoons Dijon mustard
$1/4$ cup chopped onion	salt and pepper to taste
1 clove garlic, minced	chopped parsley to garnish

Preheat oven to 350°. Pat chops dry with paper towels and sprinkle both sides with salt and pepper. Heat vegetable oil in a frying pan large enough to hold chops in a single layer, and sauté on both sides until golden, about 5 minutes a side, over medium heat. Wrap each in foil and place in the oven. Bake 30 minutes, or until tender.

Discard any fat from the frying pan and add butter. Cook onion and garlic over medium heat until onion softens, then add wine. Cook down over high heat until wine has become almost a glaze, then add cream and mustard. Whisk until you have a smooth, slightly thickened sauce. Remove chops from oven, unwrap, and place on a warm platter, then pour sauce over. Sprinkle with parsley and serve.

Adding a spirit to food while it's still cooking will cause the alcohol to evaporate quickly. What remains is flavor and aroma, it is unclear how much alcohol is retained when cooked... anywhere from 5-85%.

SAUSAGE & RICE CASSEROLE

2 pounds bulk sausage
4-5 green onions, chopped
   with tops
1 large green pepper,
   chopped
1 medium stalk celery,
   chopped with tops

1 cup raw rice
2 envelopes Lipton chicken
   noodle soup
1 cup water chestnuts, sliced

Preheat oven to 350°. Brown sausage and drain. Sauté onion, pepper and celery in sausage drippings until limp. Cook soup in 4$^1/_2$ cups of water for exactly 7$^1/_2$ minutes. Mix sausage, veggies, rice, and chicken soup all together. Pour in greased 9 x 13" casserole. Cover with foil. Bake for one hour. Uncover and bake 30 minutes more. Always a hit at family gatherings and covered dish events.

KENTUCKY HOT BROWN

sliced cooked turkey
sliced country ham
2 bread slices per person,
   toasted and cut into
   triangles (quantity depends
   on number of servings)

Parmesan cheese
cooked asparagus
tomato slices
parsley
bacon, cooked and crumbled

CHEESE SAUCE:
$^1/_4$ cup butter
2 tablespoons flour
1$^1/_2$ cups milk

1$^1/_2$ cup grated cheddar
   cheese

Make the cheese sauce; in a skillet mix all of the cheese sauce ingredients and stir slowly until thick and smooth. For one sandwich toast two slices of bread. Place one slice in center of plate, and two triangles on either end. Add one thick slice of city or country ham, white meat turkey or chicken on center slice. Pour on enough cheese sauce to cover top, and a little bit on triangles. Next, sprinkle on parmesan cheese, two slices of cooked bacon. Broil sandwich for 30 seconds to one minute, until bubbly. Add tomato slices on the end triangles of toast and two slices of cooked asparagus. Garnish with parsley.

NEW YEAR'S DAY MENU
HOPPIN' JOHN

3 slices bacon
1 small onion chopped
1 16-ounce package frozen
  or fresh black eyed peas

salt and pepper to taste
2 cups cooked rice

A traditional Southern New Year's Day menu includes Black Eyed Peas and Collard Greens, serve with Ham or Roast Pork and Corn Bread. The Pork is for good health The Black Eyed Peas are for good luck and the Collard Greens for financial prosperity... the more you eat the better New Year you'll have!

Cook bacon in skillet until crisp; remove bacon, reserving drippings in skillet. Crumble bacon and set aside. Sauté onion in bacon drippings until tender. Cook frozen or fresh black eyed peas according to directions (if using fresh: put in boiling water with 2 teaspoons butter and salt and pepper and cook until tender). Meanwhile, cook rice and set aside. Place rice in serving bowl. Add onions to peas. Pour pea mixture over rice and sprinkle with bacon.

TURNIP GREENS

2 pounds fresh turnip greens
1/2-1 cup chopped ham
4 cups water

1 tablespoon cider vinegar
1 teaspoon salt
1/4 teaspoon pepper

Wash greens, drain and tear into bite size pieces. Combine greens, ham, water and bring to a boil. Cover, reduce heat and cook for 30 minutes. Add vinegar, salt, pepper. Cover and cook one hour.

A·TABLE WITH·A·VIEW

RESTAURANTS

ALEXANDER'S BOUILLABAISSE

1½ carrots
5 celery stalks
1½ large Spanish onions
1 medium size leek
¼ small fennel bulb
1¾ ounces olive oil
½ ounce fennel seed
¼ ounce fresh garlic
3 cups canned tomatoes
   with juice

3 cups tomato juice
¼ teaspoon Spanish saffron
¾ quart spring water
1 teaspoon dried oregano ·
1 teaspoon fresh basil
   chopped
½ teaspoon crushed red
   chili peppers
1 gallon fresh white fish stock
1 quart white wine

Slice the first five ingredients, then in a large Dutch oven, lightly sauté chopped vegetables in olive oil. Add remaining ingredients and bring to a boil, reduce heat and simmer for 12 minutes. Add your favorite seafoods and simmer 15 more minutes.

ALEXANDER'S PEANUT BUTTER WITH FUDGE SAUCE PIE

5½ ounces cream cheese
13½ ounces peanut butter
5 tablespoons granulated
   sugar
2 teaspoons vanilla

2 teaspoons melted butter
¾ cup heavy cream
10" Oreo Pie Crust Shell
½ cup fudge sauce

In a large bowl cream together first five ingredients with a spatula. Fold in heavy cream. Evenly pour filling into pie crust. Freeze or refrigerate for several hours (or longer). In a saucepan or microwave warm the fudge sauce. Top pie with fudge sauce and serve immediately.

This celebrated seafood stew from Provence, is usually ladled over thick slices of French bread. The fish stock called for can be made by combining about 2 pounds of white fish bones and heads (without gills), 6 cups of water, 1 cup white wine, 1 cup celery, 1 cup onion, 1 teaspoon thyme or other herbs of choice, a bay leaf and salt and pepper to taste. Boil and simmer about 20 minutes. Strain and discard solids.

AUNT CHILADAS
HUEVOS RANCHEROS

1 1/2 cups dried black beans
2 large cloves garlic
1 canned chipotle chile in
  adobo sauce
2 quarts water
sea salt to taste
3 tablespoons lard

1 tablespoon butter
8 large eggs
6 cups Rancheros sauce
4 tablespoons sour cream
12 sprigs cilantro
2 Poblano chiles cut into
  strips

Food for thought: The poblano chile is a dark, almost black green chile with a rich flavor that varies from mild to snappy. The hot chipotle chile is actually a dried smoked jalapeño. It has a wrinkled dark brown skin and a smoky, almost chocolate-like flavor.

Place beans, garlic, and chipotle chile in a saucepan, cover with water and simmer until beans are very soft, about 1-2 hours. Drain, season with salt, and discard the chile. Melt the lard over medium heat in a heavy skillet or frying pan. Mash the beans with a potato masher or large spoon, and add to the pan. Fry until beans have a firm and smooth consistency, set aside and keep warm. Melt butter in a skillet and fry eggs, sunny side up. Spoon 1 1/2 cups of Rancheros sauce on plates and place two fried eggs on top of each serving. Crisscross strips of Poblano chiles on top of eggs. Serve beans on the side, garnish with sour cream and cilantro.

THE BEAUFORT INN
JALAPEÑO GRIT CAKES WITH
SHRIMP & TASSO SAUCE

1 tablespoon butter
24 medium shrimp, peeled
  and deveined with tails
1 cup diced tasso ham
1/2 cup heavy cream
1/2 cup grated Parmesan
  cheese

1 cup cooked hot grits
3 jalapeño peppers, finely
  diced
fresh chives, chopped

In a large skillet, melt the butter and sauté the shrimp and tasso ham on medium heat for one minute, or until shrimp turns pink. Stir in the cream and cheese. Reduce heat to simmer and cook, stirring constantly, until the sauce thickens. Set aside and keep warm. In a small bowl, mix together the hot grits and peppers and form the mixture into 4 cakes. Place one cake on each serving plate and pour the reserved sauce over the cakes. Garnish with chives and serve immediately.

THE BEAUFORT INN
RACK OF VENISON WITH SPICED
CRANBERRY & BLACK BEAN SAUCE

1 rack venison roast
1 tablespoon dried oregano
1 tablespoon dried thyme
1 tablespoon ground cumin
1/2 tablespoon ground
   coriander
3/4 teaspoon ground nutmeg

1 tablespoon freshly ground
   black pepper
1 pound unsalted butter
10 whole green onions,
   trimmed
10 cloves garlic, peeled
3/4 cup Merlot red wine

SAUCE:
1 pound fresh cranberries
1/2 cup white or apple vinegar
1 cup packed dark brown
   sugar
2 teaspoons ground
   cinnamon
1/2 teaspoon ground cloves

2 Granny Smith apples,
   cored and chopped
grated peel of 1 orange
1 pound cooked black beans
5 tablespoons chopped fresh
   cilantro
salt and black pepper to taste

Prepare sauce first: In a large saucepan, beginning with the
cranberries combine the first 7 ingredients and bring to a boil.
Reduce heat to simmer and cook for 30 minutes. Stir in the
black beans, cilantro and season to taste; heat through. Keep
warm on stove while cooking the venison. Preheat oven to
350°. Trim the fat around the eye of the roast.

In a small bowl, mix together all of the herbs and spices and
rub the mixture twice on the outside of the roast. In a large
cast-iron Dutch oven, melt the butter. When the Dutch oven is
hot, place the roast in the bottom and surround with the
onions and garlic. Sauté each side of the roast for about 3 minutes. Add the wine and bake for about 15 minutes for medium
rare. (Venison should not be cooked more than medium rare
or may lose significant amount of flavor.) Let cool slightly.
Serve with the Spiced Cranberry and Black Bean Sauce.

Located just 50 minutes from Hilton Head in charming Beaufort, South Carolina, the Beaufort Inn was originally built in 1907 as a private summer residence. Operated as a boarding house and inn for more than 50 years until 1962. In July 1994, under new ownership and boasting a second complete renovation, the local landmark was reopened as the Beaufort Inn, and has since attracted the country's and especially Hollywood's attention. Major stars filming in the Lowcountry have enjoyed the Inn's hospitality and Holland-born Chef Peter de Jong's exquisite meals.

BESS'
BEEF & MUSHROOM SOUP

5 cans cream of mushroom
    soup
1 pound mushroom slices
2 cloves of garlic, minced

5-7 cups beef consommé
1 pound chopped medium-
    rare roast beef
$1^1/_4$ cup red table wine

Sauté mushrooms and garlic until soft. In a large pot put cream of mushroom soup, filling each soup can with beef consommé, instead of water. Whisk soup. Heat to low boil, add sautéed mushrooms and beef. Season with pepper and red wine. Serves 10.

BETSY'S GOURMET TO GO
FAMOUS SWEET POTATO BISCUITS

$^3/_4$ cup mashed sweet
    potatoes
$^2/_3$ cup milk
$^1/_4$ melted butter

$1^1/_4$ cups all-purpose flour
1 tablespoon sugar
1 tablespoon baking powder
$^1/_2$ teaspoon salt

Preheat oven to 450°. Combine potatoes, milk and butter. Sift flour, sugar, baking powder and salt together. Add to potato mixture and blend into soft dough.

Place dough on lightly floured surface. Knead until surface of dough is smooth. Roll out to $^1/_2$" thickness. Cut with biscuit cutter and place on greased baking sheet. Bake for 8-10 minutes or until lightly browned. Makes 12-16 biscuits.

BOATHOUSE GRILL CORNMEAL CRUSTED CATFISH & OYSTERS

CHUTNEY:
2 pounds peaches, peeled, pitted and cubed
1 tablespoon mustard seed
1/4 teaspoon chili powder
1 teaspoon peeled and chopped fresh ginger
1 pound sugar
1 cup white vinegar
1 cup yellow mustard
1 cup yellow raisins

Boil peaches and raisins in vinegar for 20 minutes. Add sugar and boil until thick. Add the rest of the ingredients and cook 10 minutes longer, then chill.

SAFFRON RICE:
2 tablespoons butter
3 cups converted rice
1 teaspoon saffron
4 cups chicken stock
1 cup white wine
1 small onion diced
salt and pepper to taste

Melt butter, add onions and sauté until tender. Add rice and sauté for one minute with saffron. Add wine and chicken stock, salt and pepper to taste. Bring to a boil for 5 minutes, then lower flame. Cover and let steam for 15 minutes or until water is absorbed.

6 6-ounce catfish filets
36 select oysters, out of shells
2 cups fine cornmeal
1 cup flour
1 teaspoon garlic powder
1/2 teaspoon salt
1/2 teaspoon black pepper
1/4 teaspoon cayenne
2 cups buttermilk
4 eggs
oil for frying

Mix all dry ingredients in a large bowl. Mix buttermilk and eggs in another bowl. In a large frying pan, heat oil to 325°. Soak all seafood in buttermilk egg mix, then dredge in cornmeal/flour mixture. Fry catfish until golden brown, about 8 minutes. Remove catfish and keep warm in oven. Drop oysters in oil one at a time; fry until they float, about 2 minutes. Serve one fish filet and six oysters on top of rice with chutney on the side.

Chicken stock can be made by combining: 12-15 cups water, 4-5 pounds picked chicken bones, 2 cups onions, 1 cup celery, 4-5 carrots chopped, 1 bay leaf, thyme, parsley, salt and pepper. Boil. Simmer for about 1- 2 hours. Skim scum from surface periodically. Strain. If refrigerating, skim fat from top before using.

BLUFFTON OYSTER COMPANY OYSTERS ELEANOR

1 dozen raw oysters
1 dozen oyster half shells
1 cup bacon, cooked and crumbled

1 cup chopped onion
1 cup grated cheddar cheese

Cook bacon until crispy. Crumble. Sauté onions in bacon drippings until translucent. Place each oyster in a half shell. Top each oyster with cooked onion, then bacon crumbles, then cheese. Broil in oven for about 3 minutes, or until cheese melts and is bubbly. Place on bed of rock salt if desired. Serve with saltines and cocktail sauce.

CAFE AT BELFAIR POTATO-ONION CRUSTED GROUPER

1 large potato
$1/4$ onion
1 egg
$1/4$ cup cream
$1/2$ cup grated Parmesan
1 clove of garlic, minced

pinch of crushed shallot
pinch of fresh herbs
4 8-ounce grouper fillets
flour for dredging
$1/4$-$1/2$ cup oil

Shred potato and onion, squeeze out all liquid using a clean towel. Combine potato and onions with egg, cream, Parmesan and seasonings. Dredge fillet in flour, and wrap with potato mixture and chill at least one hour. Sauté in hot oil on both sides until golden. Finish in 450° oven for 7-8 minutes.

SOUR CREAM CAPER DILL SAUCE:

1 cup sour cream
$1/2$ cup heavy cream
1 tablespoon capers

$1/2$ tablespoon dill
pinch crushed shallot and garlic mixture

Mix together all ingredients and warm over low heat.

CAFE EUROPA
VIDALIA ONION TART
WITH SWEET RED PEPPER COULIS

TART:

9"-frozen pie shell
PAM non-stick spray
5 medium Vidalia onions
3 tablespoons butter
2 eggs
½ cup sour cream

¼ cup heavy cream
1 tablespoon chopped
  parsley
salt and white pepper-dash
  of each

Preheat oven to 350° Spray a 9" scalloped-edge tart pan with a removable bottom, with PAM. Remove frozen pie shell from it's aluminum pan, and press into tart pan, being sure to press into corners. Peel the onions, and cut them to make rings. Melt the butter in a large frying pan, gently sauté the onions until light brown and set aside. Gently mix together eggs, creams, parsley and salt and pepper, then pour into tart shell. Next, fill the shell with the browned onions. Bake until the crust and top are brown, about 20 minutes.

COULIS:

2 medium sweet red peppers
1 Vidalia onion
1 shallot

¼ cup white wine
salt and pepper to taste

Rub the 2 red peppers with olive oil, then roast them whole in a 350° oven until the skins turn dark. Peel, then chop the Vidalia onion and the shallot. After the roasted red peppers have cooled, peel, seed and chop them. Put the peppers, onion, shallot, white wine and salt and pepper in a food processor and blend into a sauce, being sure to puree all chunks. Serve the tart in pie-shaped pieces at room temperature, dribbled with swirls of the red pepper coulis, and garnish with a sprig of parsley.

RESTAURANTS

She-Crab soup is widely recognized as a South Carolina specialty. A distinctive difference in our state's version of this creamy favorite is the inclusion of crab roe or eggs. Since fresh roe is only available in the spring, She-Crab soup, in its purist form, is seasonal.

CAROLINA CAFE AT THE WESTIN RESORT SHE-CRAB SOUP

1 onion, diced
2 celery stalks, diced
1 pound backfin crab
1 pound crab claw meat
1/2 pound blue crab roe
   (substitute ground carrot)
salt and white pepper to taste

1 tablespoon chicken broth
mace to taste
6 ounces Harvey's Bristol
   Cream
1/2 gallon milk
3 pints heavy cream

ROUX:
4 ounces butter

4 ounces flour

A roux is used to thicken soups and sauces.

SACHET BAG:
1 teaspoon fennel seed
1 bay leaf

1 teaspoon peppercorns
parsley stem

In a large Dutch oven sauté onion and celery in the 4 ounces of butter. When onions are translucent, add flour. Cook over low heat for approximately 5 minutes. Add all other ingredients except crab meat. Simmer 20 minutes. Add crab, and adjust seasonings.

CHARLIE'S L'ETOILE VERTE PATE MAISON

5 pounds chicken livers,
   rinsed and cleaned
1 pound and 12 tablespoons
   butter
1 large white onion, chopped
6 large mushrooms, chopped

1/4 teaspoon salt
1 teaspoon black pepper
1 tablespoon dried thyme,
   whole leaf
6 tablespoons sherry

Sauté livers, onion, mushrooms, and dry ingredients in one pound of butter over low heat until well done, one hour. No pink showing in livers. Cool approximately for 30 minutes. Puree mixture in two separate batches with 6 tablespoons cold butter and 3 tablespoons of sherry added to each batch. Spoon into loaf pan lined with plastic film and level with spatula. Cover with plastic film and refrigerate overnight. Unmold and slice when ready to serve.

164

CQ'S
RASPBERRY DUCK

3 pound boneless duck breast

RASPBERRY VINAIGRETTE:

2 quarts fresh raspberries	1 tablespoon salt
1 cup rice wine vinegar	1 tablespoon pepper
1/4 cup sugar	1 tablespoon garlic
1/2 cup vegetable oil	1 small red onion

In a large bowl, mix raspberry vinaigrette (save 1 cup for later) with duck breast to marinate (chilled) for 3 hours. Grill the duck for 1 minute skin down (be careful...it will burn quickly), then turn over to cook on other side for 5 minutes on medium heat (cooking times will vary...make sure duck is cooked through). Drape the leftover raspberry vinaigrette over the duck and garnish with fresh berries. Serve with brown or wild rice and fresh steamed vegetables.

CQ'S
CITRUS CREPES WITH STRAWBERRY MOUSSE

CREPES:

2 large eggs	1/2 cup sugar
1 zest of orange	11/4 cup flour
1 zest of lime	11/2 cup milk
1 zest of lemon	4 tablespoons butter
1/4 teaspoon of salt	

STRAWBERRY MOUSSE:

2 pints strawberries	2 cups whipped cream
1/2 cup sugar	

Mix all ingredients in a bowl until smooth. Let stand 20 minutes. Pour 4 ounces of crepe batter in a teflon coated sauté pan over medium heat. Cook until brown on both sides. Place on a sheet pan to cool

Puree berries and sugar. Fold whipped cream into berry mixture. Let it cool for 10 minutes in refrigerator. Stuff citrus crepes with mousse.

As easy as they are delicious! Try it for a different summer dessert.

165

CRAZY CRAB
CRABMEAT STUFFED MUSHROOMS

1 pound crabmeat, cooked
  and shell free
1/3 cup cracker crumbs
3 tablespoons mayonnaise
1 1/2 tablespoons chopped
  parsley

1 teaspoon lemon juice
1 teaspoon Tabasco
1 pinch black pepper
1 dozen jumbo mushrooms

Preheat the oven to 350°. Remove stems from mushrooms, (if necessary, scoop out small area for crab mixture). Combine all ingredients, except the mushrooms. Stuff the mushrooms with the crabmeat mixture. Bake in oven for 10 minutes or until mushrooms are tender. Top with hollandaise or your favorite sauce.

CROWNE PLAZA RESORT
LEMON CUSTARD FRENCH TOAST WITH MAPLE PECAN BUTTER

6 whole eggs, beaten
1 cup whole milk
1 cup whipping cream
zest of 1 lemon
zest of 1 orange

2 tablespoons vanilla extract
1/2 cup sugar
1 tablespoon cinnamon
1/2 teaspoon nutmeg

Blend together all ingredients thoroughly and chill. Stir before each use. Best to use French bread or Texas toast. Dip bread in batter and cook on hot buttered griddle, turning over as needed. Serve with Maple Pecan Butter.

MAPLE PECAN BUTTER:
1/2 cup roasted pecans
1/2 cup dark brown sugar

1 pound unsalted butter

Soften butter at room temperature. Knead in pecans and sugar by hand or with mixer. Chill until firm but still workable. Refrigerate. Butter may be rolled into a log, wrapped in parchment paper and sliced off as needed.

FRATELLO'S ITALIAN RESTAURANT
CHICKEN PORTOFINO

2 full chicken breasts	4 ounces mozzarella cheese
salt and pepper to season	2 ounces Parmesan cheese
4 ounces Fratello's Italian	1 cup tomato sauce
sausage	1/2 cup white wine

Preheat oven to 425°. Cook sausage until done. While sausage is cooking, pound 2 full chicken breasts and lay out flat. Season with salt and pepper. Slice cooked Fratello's Italian sausage lengthwise and place on chicken breasts. Sprinkle mozzarella and Parmesan cheese evenly over sausage. Roll chicken lengthwise. Place chicken in baking pan and top with tomato sauce and white wine. Bake for 35 minutes. Great served with sautéed onions and peppers and a side of pasta or rice.

GIUSEPPI'S
HERITAGE BROCCOLI SALAD

2 bunches broccoli, cut into florets	2/3 cup raisins
10 slices bacon-cooked until crisp, then crumble	1/2 cup chopped onion

DRESSING:

1 cup mayonnaise	2 tablespoons vinegar
1/2 cup sugar	

In a large mixing bowl combine the first 4 ingredients. In a small bowl mix together the dressing ingredients combining thoroughly. Pour the dressing over broccoli mixture. Chill several hours until ready to serve.

This popular salad is requested during the MCI Classic golf tournament by the "Mega-Ton"

GIUSEPPI'S PIZZA & PASTA
ITALIAN WEDDING SOUP

1¹/₂ pounds ground beef
6 ounces Parmesan cheese
2 eggs
¹/₂ teaspoon salt

1 teaspoon black pepper
4 ounces frozen spinach
6 ounces orzo
1 quart chicken broth

Prepare meatballs and brown in olive oil until cooked. In a medium bowl combine Parmesan cheese, eggs, salt, and black pepper, whip ingredients together until consistent. Cook the orzo as directed on package. In a large pot bring chicken broth to a boil, add cooked meatballs, add Parmesan cheese and egg mixture stirring until dissolved into broth. Add small pieces of spinach, add noodles. Remove from heat, stir and serve.

HARBOURMASTER'S
ANGEL HAIR CRUSTED CRAB CAKES WITH PERNOD CREAM SAUCE

¹/₂ pound crabmeat, shelled and cleaned
2 whole lemons
1 teaspoon Worcestershire
white pepper

fresh dill weed
Tabasco sauce
bread crumbs
3 tablespoons mayonnaise
¹/₂ pound angel hair pasta

PERNOD CREAM SAUCE:
¹/₂ large onion, diced
4 tablespoons sour cream
3 tablespoons mayonnaise

2 tablespoons heavy cream
3 tablespoons chopped spinach

Cook pasta in hot water without any butter or oil until just under done. Cool quickly and set aside. Mix well all ingredients, vary quantity of lemons, pepper, dill weed and Tabasco sauce to taste. Add bread crumbs to bind seasonings. Make a small ball out of crab mixture, wrap in pasta. Lightly apply oil or non-stick spray to medium pan, allow oil to warm a minute then sauté crab cake until golden brown. Meanwhile for Pernod cream sauce: sauté the diced onion with Pernod, reduce heat and add sour cream and heavy cream. Stir in chopped spinach (for color) and serve with crab cakes.

"Constantly allow the child participation in our lives. For he cannot learn to act if he does not join in our actions."
— Maria Montessori

HARBOURTOWN DELI
LOWCOUNTRY OMELET

FILLING:

1 can lump crabmeat
10-12 shrimp cleaned,
    shelled, tail cut off
1/2 clove garlic minced
1/2 onion chopped

2 tablespoons butter
1-2 sprigs of dill
1/4-1/3 cup Parmesan cheese
1/3-1/2 cup heavy whipping
    cream

In large saucepan over medium-high heat, sauté onion and garlic. When soft, add crabmeat and shrimp, cook until shrimp are pink, just a couple of minutes. Lower the heat, add dill and sprinkle in Parmesan cheese. Slowly stir in the cream, continue stirring until a thick heavy sauce is formed. Put on very low heat to keep warm before adding to omelet.

OMELET:

4 eggs
1/4 milk
1/2 teaspoon salt

1/8 teaspoon paprika
1 1/2 teaspoons butter

In a medium bowl, beat the eggs with a fork until blended. Beat in the milk, salt and paprika. In a skillet or omelet pan, melt the butter. When the butter is fairly hot, add the egg mixture. Cook over low heat. Lift the edges with a pancake turner and tilt the skillet to permit the uncooked mixture to run to the bottom, or stick the egg mixture with a fork in the soft spots to permit the heat to penetrate the bottom layer. When it is an even consistency, add the "lowcountry" filling, fold the omelet over and serve immediately.

HEMINGWAY'S AT THE HYATT REGENCY
PEACH FRITTERS WITH
VANILLA PECAN CREAM SAUCE

FRITTERS:
2 cups all-purpose flour
2 tablespoons golden brown
  sugar
1 teaspoon baking powder
1/2 teaspoon salt
1/2 cup chilled unsalted butter,
  cut into small pieces

2 large peaches pitted,
  peeled and mashed
1 vanilla bean
vegetable oil for deep frying

Mix first four ingredients in processor. With machine running, add butter and process until fine crumbs form. Transfer to a large bowl. Add mashed peaches and vanilla and stir to form soft but not sticky dough. Heat oil in deep pot to 375°. Deep fry fritters in batches until crisp and golden brown on all sides, about 5 minutes. Remove to plates and pour sauce as desired.

SAUCE:
1 cup sugar
1 cup egg yolks
  (approximately 8 yolks)

1 quart cream
1 vanilla bean
1 cup chopped pecans

Pour cream in saucepan, split vanilla bean and add to cream, and heat on low, (do not boil). In a separate bowl, combine sugar and egg yolks, whip with wire whisk slowly until sugar dissolves and mixture is frothy. Remove cream from heat. Ladle small amount of cream mixture into the egg yolk sugar mixture. Combine egg yolk mixture back into cream (raising temperature of egg yolks without cooking). Blend in cream, return to heat and heat until mixture is thickened, stirring constantly (do not boil!). Strain with a fine sieve. Place cream sauce bowl in bowl of ice to cool quickly. Fold in chopped pecans.

HILTON HEAD BREWING COMPANY CRUMBLY APPLE PIE

FILLING:

7 medium Granny Smith apples, peeled, cored and sliced very thin
$^1/_2$ cup granulated sugar

1 teaspoon ground cinnamon
$^1/_4$ teaspoon ground nutmeg
$^1/_4$ teaspoon salt
9" ready made pie crust

TOPPING:

$^3/_4$ cup firmly packed dark brown sugar
$^3/_4$ cup all-purpose flour

$^1/_2$ teaspoon ground nutmeg
$^1/_3$ cup chilled butter, cut into small pieces

Preheat oven to 400°. To prepare filling, mix together all ingredients. Spoon filling into pie crust. To prepare topping, in a small bowl, mix together brown sugar, flour and nutmeg. Using 2 knives, cut butter into brown sugar mixture until coarse crumbs form. Sprinkle topping evenly over apples. Bake pie until topping is lightly browned and filling is bubbly, approximately 35 minutes. If pie is overbrowning, cover loosely with aluminum foil. Transfer to a wire rack to cool.

A happy family is but an earlier heaven.

HOFBRAUHAUS
RINDSROULADEN-BEEF ROLLS

4-5 ounce ¹/₄" thick sliced beef top round	4 slices bacon
salt and pepper	1 thinly sliced onion
oregano, thyme and basil	1 teaspoon shortening
mustard	1 teaspoon tomato paste
dill pickle, cut lengthwise into quarters	1 cup red wine
	2 cups brown sauce or Knorr's brown sauce

Pound beef, sprinkle with seasonings to taste. Spread thinly with mustard. Top with bacon slices, add onion and pickle. Roll up each slice lengthwise and secure with a toothpick. Heat shortening in skillet, add beef rolls and sauté until well browned. Add red wine, tomato paste and brown sauce. Cover and simmer for one hour or until tender. Remove toothpick. Serve rindsrouladen with red cabbage and mashed potatoes.

HUDSON'S
SEVEN DAY SLAW

This slaw gets it's name because without any mayonnaise, it will easily last seven days.

1 head cabbage	2 tablespoons sugar
2 red onions	¹/₂ tablespoon dry mustard
¹/₃ cup sugar	¹/₄ tablespoon salt
1 cup oil	¹/₄ tablespoon black pepper
1 cup vinegar	

Slice cabbage and onions thinly or shred them. In a large bowl, toss cabbage and onions with ¹/₃ cup of sugar. In a medium saucepan, combine remaining ingredients and bring to a boil. Pour boiling mixture over cabbage, let set, and in five minutes mix. Chill in refrigerator and serve on leaves of romaine lettuce.

JULEP'S
SWEET SOUTHERN VINAIGRETTE DRESSING

1/2 medium onion
1/3 cup chili sauce
1/4 cup Dijon mustard
1/2 cup apple cider vinegar

1 teaspoon salt
1 1/2 tablespoons sugar
2 cups canola oil

In a bowl of a food processor, add first six ingredients, pulse several times to combine. Through the feeder tube, stream in canola oil until all is incorporated. Keep refrigerated. Serve as a salad dressing or over sliced tomatoes.

THE KINGFISHER
GREEK STYLE GRILLED GROUPER

1 8-ounce grouper fillet
Italian salad dressing
4 tablespoons butter
1 red onion chopped
1 cup black olives
1 red bell pepper, chopped

1 can artichoke hearts
1 clove chopped garlic
4 tablespoons sherry
salt and pepper to taste
2 ounces Feta cheese

Preheat the grill. Marinate grouper in Italian dressing for 10 minutes. While fish is marinating, in a large frying pan, sauté the onion, olives, pepper and artichoke hearts in the butter. While cooking, add the garlic, sherry and salt and pepper. Let simmer for 5 minutes. Put grouper on grill for one minute, alternate direction of fish to create grill grid marks. When marking is complete, remove from grill and place in oven on a broiler pan or similar. Broil 6-8 minutes. Add Feta cheese to the sautéed mixture. Cheese will melt slightly and thicken, add lemon juice, stir gently. Pour mixture over grouper and serve with garlic mashed potatoes.

LAND'S END TAVERN SEAFOOD GUMBO

Seafood gumbo is generally associated with Cajun and Creole cooking, however, there are almost as many LowCountry versions and this one is particularly tasty!

2 cloves garlic, minced
1 bunch of celery, chopped
1 large onion, chopped
2 red bell peppers, chopped
1 green bell pepper, chopped
2 tablespoons butter
1 large can tomato paste
3 large cans diced tomatoes
6 cups water

1/2 teaspoon black pepper
1/2 teaspoon white pepper
1 tablespoon sugar
4 cups cubed grouper
2 pounds cleaned shrimp
2 cups corn kernels
  (fresh or frozen)
1 teaspoon seafood seasoning

In a deep soup pot lightly sauté the first 5 ingredients in the butter. Next, add all other ingredients, stirring after each addition. Turn heat to low and allow soup to cook for one hour. Serve as soup or over rice.

LA POLA'S PASTA PRIMAVERA

fettuccine
1/4 cup broccoli florets

1-2 cups vegetables
  cauliflower, mushrooms
  carrots, julienne pea pods

SAUCE:
4 tablespoons butter
1 clove garlic
1 cup heavy cream

1/2 cup grated Parmesan
  cheese
parsley sprigs

Place vegetables in pot of boiling water and blanch for 2 minutes. Cool in cold water bath, drain and reserve. Cook fettuccine in salted boiling water for 7-10 minutes, or until pasta is al dente (firm to the bite), drain and reserve. In a saucepan melt the butter and the garlic; let garlic season the butter, remove clove when starting to brown. Stir in cream, bring to a boil slowly, reduce heat and let simmer. Add prepared vegetables, stir and heat. To thicken sauce, add Parmesan cheese stirring constantly; as cheese melts and thickens sauce, reduce heat and prepare pasta. To heat pasta dip in simmering hot water for approximately one minute. Place pasta on plates. Adjust flavor with pepper, a tiny bit of salt it okay-Parmesan is salty. Distribute vegetables and pour sauce over top of pasta and Voila! Garnish with a sprig of parsley.

OLD FORT PUB
SALMON EN CROUTE

4 salmon fillets

6 4x6"-pieces of puffed pastry dough

CRABMEAT STUFFING:

8 ounces fresh crabmeat

3 slices white bread (no crusts) chopped into 1/4" cubes

3 teaspoons dry mustard

1/2 teaspoon salt

1/4 teaspoon white pepper

1/4 cup grated Parmesan cheese

2 tablespoons chopped fresh parsley

juice of 1 lemon

4 teaspoons Worcestershire sauce

4 teaspoons dry sherry

Preheat oven to 350°. In a large bowl combine ingredients for stuffing, mixing well. Next, arrange salmon fillets on one end of pastry dough. Top the fish with 1/2 cup of crabmeat stuffing and fold the remaining end of dough over the top of both. Pinch edges of dough by pressing with the prongs of a dinner fork. Bake for 12-15 minutes until golden brown. Finish with hollandaise sauce.

OLD OYSTER FACTORY
CHOCOLATE CREME BRULEE

4 cups heavy cream

1 teaspoon vanilla extract

8 egg yolks

3/4 cup plus 2 tablespoons sugar

4 1x1" pieces of semi-sweet chocolate

TOPPING:

4 tablespoons granulated sugar

4 tablespoons brown sugar

Preheat oven to 250°. Place chocolate chunk in center of each ramekin (or custard cups). In a large bowl carefully mix together heavy cream, sugar, egg yolks, and vanilla. Pour through fine strainer into ramekins. Place ramekins in a roasting pan filled with enough boiling water to reach halfway up sides of ramekins. Bake for about 40 minutes. In a small mixing bowl combine the sugars. Sprinkle mixture evenly over surface of each custard. Broil until sugar is caramelized. Garnish with berries and mint leaves.

"In the special environment prepared for them in our schools, the children themselves found a sentence that expressed the inner need — 'Help me do it myself!'"
— Maria Montessori

PRIMO
RICOTTA GNOCCHI

2 cups ricotta cheese	1/2 teaspoon salt
1 cup grated Parmesan cheese	1/4 teaspoon black pepper
4 egg yolks	1/8 teaspoon nutmeg
3/4 cup flour	gnocchi
	2 cups marinara sauce

Preheat oven to 400°. In a large bowl combine all ingredients, except gnocchi. Place ricotta mixture in a pastry bag without a tip. Bring a large pot of water to a slow boil. With floured fingers, pipe and pinch mixture into gnocchi dumplings. Allow to simmer 2 minutes once last gnocchi is put into the boiling water; stir very carefully if necessary. In a 9 x 13" pan spread marinara evenly to cover bottom. Remove gnocchi with slotted spoon, place on top of marinara. Cook 10 minutes to remove excess liquid. Serve immediately.

REILLEY'S
KEY LIME PIE

40 ounces Eagle brand condensed milk	9 ounces lime juice
5 egg yolks	3 ounces lemon juice
	2 graham cracker pie crusts

Beat egg yolks to the consistency of mayonnaise. Add condensed milk while beating at low speed. Add juices, continuing to beat at low speed until thoroughly mixed. Pour into pie crusts. Bake at 225° until firm, 20-25 minutes. Chill and serve.

RICK'S PLACE
BLUEBERRY BUTTERMILK BISCUITS

2 cups all-purpose flour	**dash of salt**
1/2 cup sugar	**1/4 pound unsalted butter**
2 teaspoons baking powder	**1 cup blueberries**
1/2 teaspoon baking soda	**1/2 cup buttermilk**

Preheat oven to 400°. Thoroughly combine the dry ingredients in a mixing bowl. Cut the well chilled butter into small cubes and then work it into the flour mixture smearing the butter between your thumb and fingers to combine with the flour. Do this until the butter is reduced to pea size. Add the blueberries (if you are using frozen, do NOT thaw) combining quickly. Add the buttermilk in three stages working it into the flour quickly and without kneading. The mixture should just barely hold together. You may not need all of the buttermilk. Form the dough into golf ball size drops and place on a lightly greased cookie sheet. Bake for 6-8 minutes, until done. This recipe will yield 20-24 biscuits.

RICK'S PLACE
GINGER VINAIGRETTE

3 cups peanut oil	**1 tablespoon crushed black peppercorns**
6 ounces olive oil	**1 tablespoon kosher salt**
5 tablespoons tarragon vinegar	**1/2 bunch parsley, chopped**
1/4 cup lemon juice	**2 teaspoons dried basil**
6 ounces red wine vinegar	**2 teaspoons chopped dill weed**
3 tablespoons whole grain mustard	**1 tablespoon chopped ginger**
1/2 cup bresillienne*	**1 tablespoon chopped garlic**
2 tablespoons granulated sugar	

Mix all the ingredients except the oil together in a cruet or similar with a secure top. Stir until salt dissolves. Let sit for about 30 minutes and then add the oils and combine thoroughly.

Rick and Deborah Stone have been making these little biscuits since the first day they opened and estimate they have made close to 75,000 of them over the years. The key seems to be working the dough as little as possible once you add the buttermilk. Just mix very lightly letting the dough crumble through your fingers. The result will be a light flaky biscuit.

*Bresillienne are chopped candied hazelnuts and are available at Rick's Place. You may substitute other nuts or omit them altogether.

177

SANTA FE CAFE
TEQUILA SHRIMP

20-30 large shrimp peeled
    and deveined
juice of 2 lemons
4 tablespoons butter
1/4 cup white wine
1 cup heavy cream
1 shot Tequila

1 red bell pepper julienned
1 yellow bell pepper
    julienned
1 poblano pepper, julienned
    (no seeds, no veins)
1-2 tablespoons chopped
    cilantro

GARNISH:
chopped chives
diced red bell pepper

fresh chopped cilantro
lemon and lime wedges

In a skillet, on high heat, melt 4 tablespoons butter, squeeze juice of lemons, add white wine. Add shrimp and sauté until almost cooked through (1-2 minutes). Add 1 shot glass of Tequila and very carefully flambé. Into same skillet, add heavy cream, 1-2 tablespoons chopped fresh cilantro and all peppers. Continue to cook on high heat 1-2 minutes until consistency of cream sauce reaches medium consistency. Do not overcook. Serve over red chili pasta or rice. Sprinkle plates with chives, diced pepper and fresh chopped cilantro. Garnish with lemon and lime wedges. Serves 4.

SCOTT'S FISH MARKET SAUTÈED JUMBO SHRIMP & LOBSTER MEDALLIONS

1 pound fresh fettuccine
  pasta (egg or spinach)
10 medium peeled, headed
  shrimp
10 medallions of lobster
2 tablespoons olive oil
1/4 pound Tasso ham, cut into
  thin strips
1/2 tablespoon chopped
  shallots

1/2 tablespoon minced garlic
1 tablespoon fresh thyme
1 teaspoon basil
1/2 teaspoon dill weed
2 ounces dry sherry
2 tablespoons lemon juice
1 1/2 cups heavy cream
4 tablespoons grated
  Parmesan cheese
salt and pepper to taste

Cook pasta in plain hot water while making sauce. In a large
pan, sauté shrimp and lobster in olive oil over low heat. Add
tasso ham, shallots, garlic and herbs. Increase heat to medium
high. Add sherry, lemon juice, and heavy cream. Bring to a
boil, then reduce heat. Fold in cheese. Place cooked pasta in a
serving bowl and pour sauce over the top. Serve immediately.

SIGLER'S ROTISSERIE "THE CHEF'S PLACE" PAN-SEARED TUNA MISO VINAIGRETTE WITH HOT & SOUR CABBAGE

FRESH AHI TUNA:
vegetable oil to coat
1 clove garlic, minced
1 teaspoon fresh minced
  ginger
1/8 cup chopped cilantro,
  loosely packed

Combine marinade ingredients and marinate tuna for a few hours. Pan sear on high heat until desired doneness. Serve on cabbage with vinaigrette.

SPICY MISO VINAIGRETTE:
2 tablespoons miso
  (fermented soy bean paste)
1/4 cup cider vinegar
1 teaspoon fresh minced
  ginger
1 tablespoon honey
1 tablespoon chopped spring
  onion
1 teaspoon sesame oil

In a small bowl mix together miso and vinegar until smooth. Add remaining ingredients and mix well. Chill until ready to use.

HOT & SOUR CABBAGE:
5 tablespoons sugar
1/2 cup rice wine vinegar
1 1/2 teaspoons salt
1 pound cabbage
1/4 teaspoon sesame oil
1/2 teaspoon pepper flakes

Mix sugar, vinegar and salt. Cut cabbage into thin strips, and put in a jar. In a medium to large skillet, over medium-high heat, warm oil, add pepper flakes, and stir-fry a few seconds, then turn heat off. Add sugar, vinegar, salt; stir and bring to a boil. Pour hot mixture over cabbage. Let stand overnight. Shake jar to make sure juice is absorbed evenly.

SOUTH CAROLINA YACHT CLUB CRAB & COLLARDS

1 bunch collards, chopped	1 quart heavy cream
1½ cups chopped onions	1 pound lump crabmeat
2 cloves garlic, minced	1 cup white wine
1 pint seafood stock	salt and pepper to taste

Wash collards. Sauté onion and garlic in a little clarified butter until slightly caramelized. Deglaze with white wine and add collards. Cover tightly and cook until soft. Add stock and cream. Reduce until thickened. Add crab at last minute. Season with salt and pepper. Great over buttermilk biscuits.

STELLINI ITALIAN RESTAURANT VEAL MARSALA

½ pounds veal, sliced ⅝" thick and pounded to ⅜" thick	4 tablespoons olive oil
salt	½ cup dry Marsala wine
freshly ground pepper	½ cup chicken stock
flour	2 tablespoons butter, melted

Season veal with salt and pepper, dip in flour, shake off excess. In 12" skillet, heat 4 tablespoons olive oil over moderate heat. Add veal 3 or 4 slices at a time, brown for approximately one minute on each side. Transfer veal from skillet to plate. Pour off excess oil from skillet, leaving a thin film on bottom. Add Marsala and ¼ cup chicken stock, bring to a boil. Return veal to the skillet and simmer over low heat for 5 minutes. Transfer veal to platter. Keep warm in oven. Add remaining chicken stock to sauce in skillet and boil. When sauce has reduced and has the consistency of a glaze, season to taste. Remove from the heat and stir in 2 tablespoons of melted butter. Pour over veal and serve.

Food for thought: A traditional "soul food," collard greens is a variety of cabbage and a close relative of kale. It is an excellent source of vitamins A and C, calcium and iron.

TRUFFLES
BLACK BEAN CAKES
WITH TASSO HAM & SALSA

⅓ cup tasso ham (julienned)   sour cream to garnish
2 ounces fresh tomato salsa

Place black bean cakes and ham in a lightly oiled pan. Place 2 ounces of julienned tasso beside cakes and heat under broiler for approximately 7 minutes. There is no need to turn them over. Place one cake in center of appetizer plate. Slightly overlap the other. Sprinkle Tasso ham around perimeter of plate. Spoon ¼ cup fresh salsa in center of cakes so that if falls off both sides. Garnish with sour cream, squirt zig-zag lines over both cakes. Sprinkle with sliced scallions.

These black bean cakes appear on the menu at Truffles in the appetizer column. But served with a large green salad, this dish makes a terrific entree as well.

BLACK BEAN CAKES:
1¾ pounds black beans, cooked and drained
2 tablespoons butter
1 small red onion
4 garlic cloves
2-4 jalapeño peppers, seeded
1 red bell pepper
4 egg yolks

2½ cups fresh bread crumbs
5 teaspoons Tabasco sauce
½ bunch fresh cilantro, chopped
2¼ teaspoons ground cumin
1 teaspoon fresh ground black pepper
¾ tablespoon salt

Rough chop onions, garlic and peppers and place in food processor, pulse and scrape until all vegetables are finely and evenly chopped. Drain excess juices. In a skillet, melt butter over moderate heat, Add red onion, garlic, jalapeño and red bell pepper. Cook until limp.

In a large bowl add to beans and let mixture cool. Place ¾ of the mixture in bowl of food processor. Puree for about 10-15 seconds. Remove from food processor and combine with the rest of the beans. Add egg yolks, bread crumbs, Tabasco, cilantro, cumin and black pepper. Test to see if it's stiff enough to shape, if not add a few more bread crumbs (mixture should not be sticky or gooey, but form easily without sticking to your hands.)

Shape bean mixture into 3 ounce cakes. Each cake should be 3" across and ½" thick. Lightly dredge in very fine bread crumbs, shaking off the excess. Rub vegetable oil evenly, and liberally over a full sheet pan and place in the oven for 5 minutes to heat. When heated, quickly remove pan from oven and place bean cakes on hot pan and return to the oven.

continued on next page

Bake cakes for approximately 5 minutes. Remove and turn each cake over. Return to oven for approximately 5 minutes. Remove from oven and let cakes cool thoroughly before placing in the refrigerator.

TOMATO SALSA:

1 quart tomatoes, seeded and chopped

2 fresh jalapeño peppers, finely chopped

1 red onion, finely chopped

1/2 cup fresh cilantro, chopped

1/2 tablespoon salt

3 tablespoons fresh lime juice

1 1/2 tablespoons olive oil

1/2 cup tomato puree

In a very large bowl mix all ingredients together. Store in refrigerator in airtight plastic container.

TWO ELEVEN PARK
LOWCOUNTRY PAELLA

SAUCE:

3 tablespoons olive oil
1/2 onion chopped
3 cups water
1 cup cream

1 cup grits
salt and pepper to taste
pinch of saffron

SEAFOOD:

2 tablespoons garlic
20 clams
20 mussels
1 pound scallops
1 pound shrimp, peeled and
   deveined

1 bunch parsley chopped
6 leaves basil chopped
3 tablespoons olive oil
1/2 cup white wine

In a medium saucepan, heat olive oil and onions and cook until translucent over medium heat. Add water and cream and bring to a boil. Stir in grits, salt, pepper and saffron and return to boil. Reduce heat to low and cover, stirring occasionally until done. Add water if too thick. In a separate pan heat oil and garlic. Add all seafood and white wine and bring to a boil. Reduce heat and cover for 7-10 minutes until shellfish open. Add shrimp when you have 2-3 minutes to go. To serve: divide grits among four bowls and top with seafood and fresh herbs.

DESSERTS

DESSERTS

SAVANNAH TRIFLE

1 angel food cake
1 medium jar apricot
  preserves
1 cup sherry
3 bananas, sliced
4 nectarines or peaches,
  sliced

3 cups strawberries or kiwi
  or combination
1 cup blueberries
2 small packages of cooked
  vanilla pudding (not instant)
whipped cream
raspberries

Prepare vanilla pudding according to the package instructions, using whole milk. Do not cool. Must be added to trifle while pudding is warm. Tear angel food cake in thirds. Keeping each third separate, tear the thirds apart. Put one third, torn into pieces on bottom of trifle dish. Spread 1/3 of apricot preserves across angel food cake, drizzle sherry to taste, and spread 1/3 of combined fruit on top. Repeat this process three times. The mixture should be close to the top of the trifle bowl. Pour warm vanilla pudding over the trifle and spoon through the sides so that the pudding can drip down the sides. Top with fresh whipped cream and refrigerate. Garnish with raspberries before serving. Must be served same day as prepared.

GRANDMOTHER WEESE'S APPLE ROLL

4 eggs with pinch of salt
1 cup sugar
2 tablespoons boiling water

1 cup flour
1 teaspoon baking soda
2 cups applesauce

Preheat oven to 350°. Beat eggs until light, mix in the other ingredients except applesauce in order as listed, mix well. Pour into greased, floured jelly roll pan. Bake for 15 minutes. Turn onto sugared cloth, spread quickly with applesauce, and very quickly roll, jelly roll style. Trim the ends and refrigerate. Slice and serve.

Historic Savannah. The only major Southern town to survive Sherman's march and a port city rich in tradition and Southern hospitality. Just a 50 minute drive from Hilton Head and a day trip worth the effort Try lunch at Mrs. Wilke's Boarding House, a narrated horse and carriage tour of downtown, a walk and shop down cobblestone-clad River Street or an evening at the Savannah Symphony! An enchanting diversion.

MAXINE'S OLD FASHIONED SKILLET CHOCOLATE MERINGUE PIE

1 1/2 cups sugar
3 tablespoons flour
3 tablespoons cocoa
3 tablespoons butter

dash salt
1 1/2 cups milk
3 egg yolks beaten
9" baked pie shell

Preheat oven to 400°. Combine all above ingredients except pie shell. Cook in a heavy pan (black iron skillet is best), over medium heat until thick. Bring to a slow boil. Pour into a baked pie shell. Top with meringue (recipe follows) and brown in oven. Good served warm.

BEST MERINGUE:
4 egg whites
1 tablespoon ice water

1/4 teaspoon cream of tartar
3/4 cup sugar

Pour egg whites and cold water into mixing bowl. Beat with mixer on high until frothy. Add cream of tartar. Beat until eggs begin to get stiff, but not dry. You will begin to see imprints of beater. Add sugar very slowly, and beat until sugar has dissolved. Top pie and brown at 400°. Meringue browns quickly so stand and watch it. Remove from oven immediately after browning.

MAXEY'S BROWNIE PIE

3 egg whites
dash of salt
3/4 cup sugar
3/4 cup fine chocolate wafer crumbs

1/2 cup chopped nuts
1/2 teaspoon vanilla
9" pie shell
whipped cream

Preheat oven to 325°. Beat egg whites with a dash of salt until soft peaks form. Add sugar and beat until stiff, fold in chocolate wafer crumbs and nuts and vanilla. Put into pie shell bake for 35 minutes. Chill 3-4 hours. Spread whipped cream on top, sprinkle wafer crumbs or chocolate curls to garnish.

COCONUT CRUNCH TORTE

½ cup flaked coconut
1 cup graham crackers,
   crushed (13 crackers)
½ cup chopped walnuts
4 egg whites

¼ teaspoon salt
1 cup sugar
1 teaspoon vanilla
9" pie shell
whipped cream

Preheat oven to 350°. Combine coconut, graham crackers and walnuts, set aside. In separate bowl beat together egg whites, salt, sugar and vanilla until stiff peaks form. Fold coconut mixture into egg whites. Pour into pie shell; bake for 30 minutes. Cool. Top with whipped cream.

AMAZING COCONUT PIE

1¾ cups milk
¾ cup sugar
½ cup Bisquick mix
4 eggs

¼ cup butter or margarine,
   melted
1½ teaspoons vanilla
1 cup flaked coconut

Preheat oven to 350°. Combine all ingredients except coconut in electric blender. Blend on low for 3 minutes. Pour into greased 9" pie pan. Let stand five minutes. Sprinkle with coconut. Bake for 40 minutes. Test with knife for doneness. Serve warm or cold. Refrigerate remaining pie.

MARGIE'S CHESS PIE

3 eggs
1½ cups sugar
1 tablespoon corn meal
1 tablespoon vinegar

1 teaspoon vanilla
6 tablespoons butter
9" pie shell

Preheat oven to 400°. Combine all ingredients except pie shell; mix until size of peas. Put into pie shell. Bake for 5 minutes, then at 325° for 30 minutes. Check for doneness by inserting a knife. If knife comes out clean, pie is ready.

BLUEGRASS PIE

9" pie crust
2 eggs
1 cup sugar
1/2 cup all-purpose flour
1/2 cup butter, melted and cooled
1 cup chocolate chips or 1/2 cup each of chocolate & butterscotch chips

1 cup chopped pecans
1 tablespoon bourbon (optional, to taste)
1 teaspoon vanilla (add more vanilla if no bourbon)

Preheat oven to 350°. Beat eggs on high until light and lemon colored. Gradually beat in sugar. Reduce speed to low and add flour and butter. Mix thoroughly. Stir in chips, nuts and flavorings. Pour into pie shell. Bake 40-50 minutes.

HERSHEY CHOCOLATE BAR PIE

6 regular-size Hershey bars with almonds
17 marshmallows, quartered
1/2 cup milk

1 cup whipped cream
9" graham cracker crust

Melt Hershey bars, marshmallows and milk in a double boiler. Let cool, then add whipped cream. Pour into a 9" graham cracker crust and place in refrigerator. Serve with a small amount of shaved chocolate, a dollop of whipped cream and a raspberry.

CHEESECAKE PIE

12 ounces cream cheese
2 eggs
3/4 cup sugar
1 teaspoon vanilla
1 1/2 cups sour cream

3 tablespoons sugar
1 teaspoon vanilla
9" graham cracker crust
raspberries

Preheat oven to 350°. Mix together first 4 ingredients. Pour cream cheese mixture into graham cracker crust; bake for 20 minutes or until set. Meanwhile, mix together sour cream, sugar and vanilla. Pour this mixture over cream cheese mixture and bake 10 minutes more. Chill thoroughly, preferably overnight.

190

IT'S A CINCH PEANUT BUTTER ICE CREAM PIE

½ gallon vanilla ice cream
2 cups crunchy peanut butter

1 can chocolate frosting
9"graham cracker pie crust

Mix peanut butter into softened ice cream. Fill pie crust with mixture and place in freezer until frozen. When pie is frozen, spread on chocolate frosting. Eat immediately.

NEVER FAILS SOUTHERN PECAN PIE

1 tablespoon butter
½ cup sugar
1 cup dark Karo syrup
4 eggs

1 cup whole pecans
pinch of salt
1 teaspoon vanilla
9" pie shell

Preheat oven to 300°. Cream butter and sugar well. Add syrup and well beaten eggs. Add pecans, salt and vanilla. Pour into pie crust and bake for 50 minutes.

CARAMEL PECAN PIE

36 caramels
¼ cup water
¼ cup margarine
¾ cup sugar
3 eggs, beaten

½ teaspoon vanilla
¼ teaspoon salt
1 cup pecan halves
9" pie shell

Preheat oven to 350°. Melt caramels with water and margarine in saucepan over low heat. Stir frequently until sauce is smooth. Combine sugar, eggs, vanilla and salt. Gradually add caramel sauce; mix well. Stir in nuts; pour into pastry shell. Bake 45-50 minutes. Pie filling will appear to be very soft, but becomes firm as it cools.

Food for thought: Store nuts in the refrigerator in airtight containers. Nuts contain oils that keep them fresh, and cool or freezing temperatures prevent the oil from oxidizing.

PARADISE PUMPKIN PIE

8 ounce package cream
  cheese, softened
$1/4$ cup sugar
$1/2$ teaspoon vanilla
1 egg
9" pie shell
$1 1/4$ cups canned pumpkin
dash salt

1 cup evaporated milk
$1/2$ cup sugar
2 eggs, slightly beaten
1 teaspoon cinnamon
$1/4$ teaspoon ginger
$1/4$ teaspoon nutmeg
maple syrup

Preheat oven to 350°. Combine softened cream cheese, sugar and vanilla, mixing until well blended. Add egg, mix well. Spread onto bottom of pastry shell. Combine remaining ingredients except syrup; mix well. Carefully pour over cream cheese mixture. Bake for 1 hour and 5 minutes. Cool. Brush with maple syrup.

TABBY APPLE PIE

2 cups whole wheat flour
2 cups all-purpose white flour
pinch of salt
1 teaspoon sugar
$1/2$ cup sweet butter
$1/2$ cup or more ice water
10 large Roma or cooking
  apples

1 cup honey
1 teaspoon apple pie spice
$1/4$-$1/3$ cup brown sugar
$1/3$ cup whole wheat flour
$1/3$ cup bourbon (optional)
$1/4$ cup sweet butter
10" fluted edge pie pan

Preheat oven to 375°. Sift together flour, salt and sugar; cut in $1/2$ cup butter with 2 knives; add ice water and blend with fork until crumbly texture is achieved; add more water if necessary until you can form dough. DO NOT OVERHANDLE IT. Divide dough in 2, roll out on floured board; place 1 pie shell in pie pan, and set aside the other shell. Peel and slice apples into mixing bowl, add honey to apples. In another bowl combine apple pie spice, brown sugar, and flour. Then add to apple mixture, add bourbon if desired. Pour apple mixture into pie pan. Cut remaining 4 tablespoons butter into small pieces on top of apples. Roll out remaining dough and place on top of apples. Flute edges with thumb and forefinger. Prick top with fork in several places. Bake at 375° for 15 minutes and then 350° for 35-40 minutes or until edges of pie are slightly brown. Ovens vary so watch the pie.

MY MAMA'S APPLE PIE

TOPPING:

½ cup all-purpose flour
⅓ cup sugar

⅓ cup butter, softened

FILLING:

½ cup sugar
½ cup firmly packed brown
  sugar
2 tablespoons all-purpose flour
¼ teaspoon cinnamon
¼ teaspoon nutmeg
⅛ teaspoon ginger
⅛ teaspoon allspice

2 teaspoons freshly grated
  orange peel
2 tablespoons orange juice
7 to 8 medium cooking
  apples (Granny Smith)
  peeled, cored and thinly
  sliced
9" pie shell

Preheat oven to 425°. Combine topping ingredients and mix with pastry blender or fork until coarse; set aside. Combine remaining ingredients and mix to coat apples. Pour into pie shell and top with crumb topping. Bake for 10 minutes at 425°, then 350° for 40-50 minutes.

Heal the past;
live the present;
dream the future.

RASPBERRY IN A CLOUD PIE

1 cup sugar
⅓ cup all-purpose flour
2 large eggs, lightly beaten
1⅓ cups sour cream
1 teaspoon vanilla extract
3 cups fresh raspberries
9" pie shell

⅓ cup all-purpose flour
⅓ cup firmly packed brown
  sugar
⅓ cup chopped pecans
3 tablespoons butter,
  softened

GARNISHES:

whipped cream

fresh raspberries

Preheat oven to 400°. Combine 1 cup sugar, ⅓ cup flour and next 3 ingredients, stirring until smooth. Gradually fold in raspberries. Spoon into pastry shell. Bake for 30-35 minutes. Combine ⅓ cup flour and next 3 ingredients; sprinkle this mixture over hot pie. Bake again at 400° for 10 minutes, until golden. Garnish . You may use frozen raspberries, but fresh are the best!

WHITE CHOCOLATE RASPBERRY TART

1 1/4 cups finely chopped
   walnuts
3/4 cup unsalted butter,
   softened
3 tablespoons sugar
1 1/2 cups all-purpose flour
1 teaspoon freshly grated
   orange zest

1 large egg beaten lightly
3 cups fresh raspberries
12 ounces white chocolate,
   chopped
1/2 cup heavy cream, warmed
1/2 cup whipped cream as
   garnish

A small seed
sometimes
produces a
large tree.
A small seed,
properly sown,
sometimes
produces a large
and fruitful tree.

In a bowl with an electric mixer blend walnuts, 1/2 cup butter, sugar, flour, zest and egg until combined. Press mixture into a 10" tart pan with removable bottom. Freeze shell 15 minutes. While shell is freezing, preheat oven to 375°. Bake shell in middle of oven 25-30 minutes, or until golden brown. Cool shell on a rack. Remove side of pan and transfer shell to a plate. Fill shell with 2 1/2 cups raspberries. In a large metal bowl set over a saucepan of barely simmering water, melt chocolate. Remove bowl from heat and whisk in cream and remaining 1/4 cup butter, whisking until smooth. Spread chocolate mixture over raspberries smoothing top, and chill, covered, 3 hours or overnight. Garnish tart with whipped cream and remaining 1/2 cup raspberries. Serve tart at room temperature.

PEACH COBBLER

¾ cup flour
1 cup sugar
2 teaspoons baking powder
dash of salt

¾ cup milk
6 tablespoons butter
2 cups peaches
1 cup sugar

Preheat oven to 350°. Combine into a batter the flour, 1 cup sugar, baking powder, salt and milk. In pie pan or other deep cooking container, melt butter. Pour batter into middle of the melted butter (don't stir). In a separate bowl, toss the peaches in the remaining 1 cup of sugar. Pour the peaches into the middle of the batter (again don't stir). Bake for one hour. Serve warm or cold with or without cream. Frozen peaches may be substituted for fresh.

SUMMER LEMON DESSERT

juice of 2 lemons
rind of 1 lemon
graham cracker crumbs to
   cover bottom of dish

1 large can Carnation
   evaporated milk, chilled
1 cup sugar

Cover glass pie dish with graham cracker crumbs and press. Beat milk until thick, then add sugar, rind and juice. Pour over graham cracker crumbs in a glass dish. Sprinkle crumbs on top of mixture. Serve immediately or chill and serve.

THE BEST BIRTHDAY CAKE FROSTING

½ cup water
1½ tablespoons corn syrup
1½ cups sugar
½ teaspoon cream of tartar

½ teaspoon salt
2 egg whites
1½ teaspoons vanilla

Place water, corn syrup, sugar, cream of tartar, and salt in a saucepan. Stir over medium heat until sugar is dissolved, forming a syrup. Place egg whites in bowl. Using a wire whip, turn to speed 10 and whip until egg whites begin to hold their shape, about 45 seconds. Continuing on speed 10 gradually add hot syrup in a thin, steady stream, about 1 to 1½ minutes. Add vanilla and continue whipping about 5 minutes or until frosting loses its gloss and stands in stiff peaks. Use immediately.

Use a countertop mixer for optimum frosting fluffiness. Add food coloring drop by drop until you achieve desired color Yield 3 cups.

CONQUEROR CORDILLO LEMON CAKE

1 package Duncan Hines
   lemon supreme cake mix or
   similar (no pudding in mix)
1 small box instant lemon
   pudding

1 cup water
1/2 cup vegetable oil
4 eggs
1 cup chopped walnuts

ICING:
1/3 cup orange juice   2/3 cup sugar

Preheat oven to 375°. Beat all ingredients together until thoroughly mixed, adding walnuts last. Bake for one hour in an ungreased tube pan. Let cool 15 minutes then remove to wire rack. Mix together orange juice and sugar; drizzle icing over warm cake.

STRAWBERRY TALL CAKE

Food for thought:
For a tangier
frosting, substitute
lemon juice for
the orange juice.

1 box white or yellow cake
   mix
1/2 cup oil
1 3-ounce box of strawberry
   Jello

1/2 cup water
1 10-ounce package frozen
   strawberries, thawed and
   mashed
4 eggs

FROSTING:
1 box confectioners' sugar
1/2 the strawberries

1/4 cup of margarine
1 teaspoon vanilla

Preheat oven to 350°. To cake mix, add 1/2 cup oil, box of Jello, 1/2 cup water, and half of the strawberries. Mix well. Add eggs one at a time beating well after each addition. Divide batter into three 8"cake pans. Bake for 25-30 minutes. While cake is baking, make frosting. Mix one box of confectioners' sugar, remaining half of strawberries, margarine and 1 teaspoon vanilla. Beat together until it is a good consistency. You may need to add more confectioners' sugar to thicken it. Let cakes cool completely before frosting. Frost this 3 layer cake as you would a 2 layer cake.

BETTER THAN
GERMAN CHOCOLATE CAKE

1 box yellow cake mix
  (no pudding in mix)
1 small box instant vanilla
  pudding
1/2 cup water
1/2 cup oil
4 eggs

1 8-ounce carton sour cream
1 6-ounce package chocolate
  chips
1 cup chopped pecans
1 bar German chocolate,
  melted
1 cup shredded coconut

Preheat oven to 350°. In a large bowl, mix first 4 ingredients; add eggs one at a time, beating well after each addition. Add next 5 ingredients, mix thoroughly Pour batter into a well greased tube pan. Bake for 50 to 55 minutes.

GOOEY CAKE SQUARES

1 box yellow cake mix
1/2 cup melted butter
1 egg

1 box confectioners' sugar
8 ounces cream cheese
2 eggs

Preheat oven to 350°. Mix first 3 ingredients. Press into bottom of greased 9 x 13" cake pan, set aside. Beat together next 3 ingredients for 5 minutes. Pour over mix in pan. Bake for 30 to 40 minutes. When cool, sprinkle with powdered sugar.

HOMEMADE IN A HURRY!

1 package Chocolate Chunk
  Brownie mix
1 container prepared white
  icing

colored sprinkles
Maraschino cherries, halves

Prepare brownies according to package directions. Pour into mini muffin pans. Bake approximately 25 minutes. When cool frost cakes and top with sprinkles and a cherry half. Fast and delicious.

MARTHA'S "SOCK IT TO ME" CAKE

1 box Golden Butter cake mix	1 cup sour cream
1/2 cup sugar	1 cup chopped pecans
3/4 cup vegetable oil	1 teaspoon almond extract
4 eggs	2 tablespoons brown sugar
	2 teaspoons cinnamon

Preheat oven to 325°. Mix together cake mix, sugar, oil, eggs and sour cream. Blend well. Stir in nuts and almond extract. Combine brown sugar and cinnamon and set aside. Pour half of batter into a greased and floured bundt pan. Sprinkle sugar mixture over batter and pour in remaining batter. Bake for one hour and 5 minutes. Cool at least 10 minutes before removing from pan. Continue to cool on wire rack.

SPICE PLUM CAKE

2 cups sugar	1 cup chopped nuts
1 cup vegetable oil	1 small jar plum baby food
3 eggs	1 teaspoon cinnamon
2 cups self-rising flour	1/2 teaspoon cloves

GLAZE:

1/2 cup confectioners' sugar	1-3 tablespoons lemon juice

Preheat oven to 350°. Place all ingredients in a large bowl and mix well. Pour into a greased and floured tube pan. Bake for one hour. Combine confectioners' sugar and lemon juice to desired consistency, may add more or less of both ingredients. Drizzle glaze on cake when cool.

SALLY'S SEA PINES CARROT CAKE

4 eggs
2½ cups unsifted all-purpose
   flour
2 tablespoons wheat germ
2 cups sugar
2 teaspoons ground cinnamon

2 teaspoons baking soda
1 teaspoon salt
1½ cups vegetable oil
3-4 jars carrot baby food
½ cup chopped walnuts

CREAM CHEESE FROSTING:
3 ounce package cream
   cheese, room temperature
4 tablespoons butter or
   margarine, softened

1¾ cups confectioners' sugar
¼ teaspoon pure vanilla
   extract

Preheat oven to 350°. Grease 10 x 15" pan. In large bowl, beat eggs at medium speed with electric mixer. Add flour, wheat germ, sugar, cinnamon, baking soda, salt, oil and carrots. Beat at low speed to combine, then at high speed until well mixed. Stir in walnuts. Spread batter smoothly in pan. Bake 30-35 minutes, until toothpick inserted in center comes out clean. Cool completely on wire rack. While cake is cooling, in small bowl combine frosting ingredients, beat at low speed to mix, then at high speed to blend. Frost cake with Cream Cheese Frosting. Cut into 1½ x 3" bars.

Sally Humphrey served as the first Headmistress at the Sea Pines Montessori School. She loved to bake bread and cakes. We're happy that her daughter, Jennifer Cauble, a Sea Pines Montessori School teacher and parent, has shared this recipe with us.

GREENBRIER HOTEL PUMPKIN CAKE

4 eggs	2 cups cake flour
2 cups sugar	2 teaspoons baking powder
1 cup vegetable oil	1 teaspoon salt
2 cups canned pumpkin	2 teaspoons cinnamon

Preheat oven to 325°. Beat eggs and sugar together until light and fluffy. Blend in oil, then pumpkin, mixing well. Add flour, baking powder, salt and cinnamon, blend well. Pour batter into greased and floured 10" tube pan or two 9" cake pans. Bake 25-35 minutes in 9" cake pans. In tube pan bake 50-60 minutes.

FROSTING:
1½ cups whipping cream   powdered sugar to taste

GARNISH:
1/4 cup graham cracker crumbs

Frost with whipping cream, garnish with graham cracker crumbs, sprinkled over top of frosting.

LONE STAR CAKE

2 cups flour	2 eggs beaten
2 cups sugar	1 cup butter
1 teaspoon baking soda	1 cup water
1/2 cup sour cream	4 tablespoons cocoa

FROSTING:

1 stick butter	1 tablespoon vanilla
1/4 cup cocoa	1 box powdered sugar
1/4 cup milk	1½ cups chopped nuts

Preheat oven to 350°. Sift together flour, sugar and soda put in a large bowl. In a medium saucepan bring the butter, water and cocoa to boil, set aside to cool. Add sour cream and eggs to dry ingredients. Next add butter and cocoa mixture. Pour into greased and floured 11 x 15" jelly roll pan (shallow). Bake for 20 minutes. Meanwhile, make frosting; in saucepan, heat butter, cocoa, milk and vanilla. Remove to a bowl and beat in powdered sugar and nuts. Frost cake when almost cool.

Food for thought: If you're in a bind, substitute all-purpose flour for cake flour. 1 cup all-purpose flour in place of 1 cup plus 2 tablespoons cake flour. All-purpose flour contains more gluten forming proteins. Gluten gives bread dough elasticity. Cakes are supposed to be more tender, so the less protein in the flour, the better.

MAMMA JACKIE'S CHEESECAKE WITH TERI'S CRUST

CRUST:

1 cup graham cracker crumbs

3 tablespoons sugar

1/4 cup melted butter

1/2 cup chopped pecans

CHEESECAKE:

3-8 ounce packages cream cheese, softened

3/4 cup sugar

3 eggs

1 teaspoon vanilla

TOPPING:

1 pint sour cream

3 teaspoons vanilla

6 tablespoons sugar

Preheat oven to 325°. Mix crust ingredients and press in the bottom of a 10" springform pan. Bake 10 minutes and cool. Preheat oven to 375°. Mix cheesecake ingredients, adding one egg at a time and mixing well. Pour mixture into cool crust and bake for 25 minutes. Allow to cool. Preheat oven to 450°. Combine topping ingredients, and pour over top of cooled cake. Bake for 5 minutes. Allow to cool before serving. Must be refrigerated.

The children bring us laughter and the children bring us tears; they string our joys like jewels bright, upon the thread of years.

SWEET TOOTH CHEESECAKE TARTS

CRUST:

1 cup Oreo cookie crumbs

3 tablespoons sugar

2 tablespoons melted butter

FILLING:

1 8-ounce package cream cheese, softened

3/4 cup sugar

3 eggs, separated

1 8-ounce carton sour cream

2 1/2 tablespoons sugar

1 teaspoon vanilla

8 ounces strawberries, sliced

Preheat oven to 350°. Mix together Oreo crumbs, sugar and butter. Press into mini muffin tins lined with cups. In another bowl, beat together cream cheese and sugar. Add egg yolks one at a time, beating well. In another bowl, combine egg whites and beat until stiff peaks form. Fold into cream cheese mixture. Spoon filling into crust, 3/4 full. Bake for 15 minutes. Remove from oven and cool. (Cakes will sink slightly). Mix together the sour cream, sugar and vanilla. Dollop a teaspoon on top of each cake. Turn oven to 400° and bake 5 minutes. Top with sliced strawberries.

Makes about 48 tasty treats, great for dessert, brunch or tea time!

CHOCOLATE VOLCANO POUND CAKE

1½ cups butter	6 eggs
8 ounces cream cheese	1 tablespoon vanilla
3 cups of sugar	3 cups sifted flour

In a large bowl, with an electric mixer cream together butter, cream cheese and sugar until fluffy. Add the very fresh eggs, one at a time, mixing between each addition. Next, stir in the vanilla. Slowly mix in the flour. Pour the batter into a greased and floured tube or bundt pan and place in a cold oven, set oven to 300° along with a cup or so of water in a separate oven-proof dish. This will keep the cake from rising too fast and keeps the texture dense. Bake for about 1 hour 15 minutes to 1 hour 30 minutes. It will depend on your oven as well as the weather. Do not overcook! The cake is best with a little "sad" streak through it. Let stand 10 minutes then invert onto a cake plate.

CHOCOLATE LAVA ICING:

½ cup butter	⅓ cup milk
⅓ cup cocoa	1 ½ teaspoons vanilla
2 cups powdered sugar	

In a medium saucepan, on low heat melt butter, then stir in cocoa, powdered sugar, milk and vanilla. Heat, mix and stir until smooth. Slowly drizzle the icing around the hot cake, letting some drip down the sides. (Not too much or it will get all over the cover of the cake plate). With the rest of the icing, fill up the hole like a volcano. YUMMY!

AWARD WINNING CHOCOLATE POUND CAKE

1 cup butter	3 cups all-purpose flour
1/2 cup shortening	1/2 teaspoon baking powder
3 cups sugar	1/2 teaspoon salt
5 eggs	1/2 cup cocoa
1 teaspoon vanilla	1 cup whole milk

Preheat oven to 325°. Cream butter, shortening and sugar. Add eggs one at a time, beating after each addition. Add vanilla. Alternately add combined dry ingredients and milk to creamed mixture. Bake in greased and floured 10" tube pan for 1 hour and 20 minutes. Cool for 3 hours before flipping onto plate.

BLACK BOTTOM CUPCAKES

1 1/2 cups flour	1 cup water
1 cup sugar	1 tablespoon vinegar
1 teaspoon baking soda	1 teaspoon vanilla
1/4 cup cocoa	1/3 cup oil
1/2 teaspoon salt	

TOPPING:

1 8-ounce package cream cheese	1/8 teaspoon salt
1 egg beaten	1 12-ounce package semi-sweet chocolate chips
1/3 cup sugar	

Sift together all the dry ingredients. Add water, vinegar, vanilla, oil and mix well. Line cupcake tins with paper baking cups and fill 1/3 full. In a medium bowl, combine cream cheese, egg, sugar and salt and beat well. Stir in chocolate chips. Top each with spoonful of cream cheese mixture. Bake at 350° for 25-35 minutes. Do not overbake.

DIRT CAKE

1 16-ounce package Oreo
1 8-ounce package cream
  cheese
1/4 cup margarine
1 cup powdered sugar
1 12-ounce Cool Whip

2 3^1/$_2$-ounce boxes instant
  vanilla pudding
3 cups milk
1 teaspoon vanilla
Clean new 8" Flower Pot

Crush cookies in blender, set aside. Mix cream cheese and margarine until smooth, mix in powdered sugar. Fold Cool Whip into cream cheese mixture. In a separate bowl combine pudding, milk and vanilla. Stir pudding mixture into cream cheese mixture. To prepare flower pot; put plastic lid over holes in the bottom of the pot, or cover with plastic wrap or use whole Oreos to cover holes. Place a layer of cookie crumbs on the bottom of flower pot, next a layer of pudding/cream cheese mixture, repeat several times, ending with cookie crumbs on top. Refrigerate. Just before serving place artificial flowers with clean stems in center of pot. Use clean new trowel to serve. For children over 3 add gummy worms in the dirt. Can be made in Dixie cups for individual servings.

Children are not things to be molded but things to be unfolded.

HEAVENLY HEATH BAR CAKE

1 box angel food cake mix
12 Heath bars, crushed
1 jar of butterscotch or
  caramel syrup (ice cream
  topping)

2 pints whipping cream,
  whipped

Prepare angel food cake as directed on package. Slice angel food cake horizontally into 3 sections. Place bottom layer on cake plate. In a large mixing bowl fold syrup into whipped cream until just mixed. Spread 1/3 of this mixture on bottom layer, then sprinkle with Heath Bar crumbs. Repeat with each layer. Top with mounds of whipped cream mixture and Heath Bar crumbs. Chill; must be refrigerated.

FROZEN LEMON SOUFFLE WITH RASPBERRY COULIS

LEMON SOUFFLE:

1 envelope unflavored gelatin
1/2 cup lemon juice
3 eggs, separated
3/4 cup sugar, divided

2 teaspoons grated lemon rind
1/8 teaspoon salt
1 cup whipping cream

In a small nonreactive saucepan sprinkle gelatin over lemon juice. Let stand 1 minute. Cook over low heat, stirring until gelatin dissolves. Set aside. Beat egg yolks and 1/4 cup sugar in a large bowl at medium speed until thick and lemon colored. Add gelatin mixture, remaining 1/2 cup sugar and grated lemon rind, stirring well. Beat room temperature egg whites and salt until stiff peaks form. Gently fold egg whites and whipped cream into lemon mixture. Spoon into 1 quart souffle dish, cover and freeze.

RASPBERRY COULIS:

1 pint fresh raspberries
1/4 cup water

1/ tablespoon lemon juice
1/2 cup sugar

In a food processor or blender combine raspberries, water and lemon juice. Puree. Strain, discarding the seeds. Pour the puree into a nonreactive saucepan and add the sugar. Bring to a boil over medium heat; reduce heat and simmer 10 minutes. Refrigerate until ready to serve.

RASPBERRY MERINGUE LADYFINGER CAKE

2 10-ounce packages frozen raspberries (or 2 1/2 cups fresh, sugar to taste)
1 1/4 cups sugar
1/3 cup water
1 teaspoon light corn syrup
4 egg whites

2 tablespoons Kirsch (optional)
2 cups whipping cream
1 package Ladyfingers (about 2 dozen split)
raspberries for garnish

In a blender puree raspberries. Press pureed raspberries through a wire strainer to remove seeds. If using fresh raspberries add sugar to taste. Combine the 1 1/4 cups sugar, water and corn syrup in a small saucepan. Bring to a boil and cook over high heat until temperature reaches 238° (soft ball stage) on a candy thermometer. In a large mixing bowl, beat egg whites until soft peaks form then gradually beat in hot syrup. Continue beating at high speed for 8 minutes or until meringue mixture cools to room temperature. Fold in raspberry puree, and Kirsch. In a separate bowl whip cream until stiff. Fold cream into meringue.

Line the buttered sides of a 9" springform pan with the split ladyfingers. Pour the raspberry mixture into the pan. Cover and freeze until firm (8 hours or longer). To serve, remove pan sides, garnish the top with fresh raspberries and slice as desired.

"The child is mysterious and powerful and contains within himself the secret of human nature."
— Maria Montessori

COOKIES
AND GOODIES

COOKIES & GOODIES

SAND DOLLAR TARTS

**1/2 pound butter, softened
1/2 cup sifted confectioners'
sugar
2 cups sifted cake flour**

**1 cup chopped pecans
1 teaspoon vanilla
1/2 cup powdered sugar**

Preheat oven to 325°. Cream butter and sugar. Stir well and add flour, nuts and vanilla. Shape into balls or crescents and bake on ungreased cookie sheet for 20 minutes or until light brown. Roll in powdered sugar while warm.

MAGGIE'S BAKERY SUGAR COOKIES

**1/2 cup shortening
1/2 cup margarine
2 cups sugar
1 teaspoon vanilla(substitute
lemon extract for a nice
summertime cookie)**

**1/2 teaspoon salt
1 teaspoon cream of tartar
3 egg yolks
2 cups flour
1 teaspoon baking soda
decorative sprinkles**

Preheat oven to 350°. Cream shortening, margarine, sugar and vanilla together. Next add salt, cream of tartar and egg yolks; mix thoroughly. Add flour and baking soda and mix until all flour is absorbed; (dough will be crumbly) Roll into balls; then roll in sugar. Place on greased cookie sheet. Bake 10 minutes, until golden around edges.

SOUR CREAM SUGAR COOKIES

**4 cups flour
1 teaspoon baking powder
1/2 teaspoon baking soda
1/2 teaspoon salt
1/2 teaspoon nutmeg**

**1 cup butter, softened
1 1/2 cups sugar
1 egg
1/2 cup sour cream
1 teaspoon vanilla**

Sift together flour, baking powder, baking soda, salt and nutmeg, set aside. In separate bowl, beat butter, sugar and egg together; add sour cream and vanilla, mix thoroughly. Mix in flour mixture. Refrigerate overnight. Preheat oven to 375°. Roll out dough about 1/4" thick and cut out with cookie cutter shapes. Bake for 10-12 minutes. Decorate as desired. For a chewy cookie, remove cookies when the edges just turn brown.

Holidays and special occasions just aren't the same without homemade cookies. For quick decorating, substitute colored "sprinkles" instead of sugar coating. Look for sprinkles made in special holiday shapes and colors too!

HERMITS

1 cup butter, softened
1½ cup brown sugar
3 eggs
1 tablespoon molasses
1 tablespoon grated orange
    peel
1 teaspoon cloves
1 teaspoon salt

1 teaspoon cinnamon
½ teaspoon ground ginger
3 cups all-purpose flour
1 teaspoon baking soda
1 cup chopped walnuts
½ cups chopped raisins
1 cup chopped dates

Preheat oven to 375°. Place butter, brown sugar, eggs, molasses, orange peel, cloves, salt, cinnamon and ground ginger in bowl. Beat with electric mixer at medium speed for one minute. Stop and scrape bowl and mix for 30 seconds more. Add flour and baking soda. Beat on low for 15 seconds. Stop and scrape bowl. At stir speed, add walnuts, raisins and dates, mixing until just blended. Drop by teaspoonfuls onto greased baking sheets. Bake 12-14 minutes. Cool on wire racks.   Makes 4 dozen cookies.

LEMON LUSTER BUTTER COOKIES

1¼ cups granulated sugar
2 cups butter
1 egg

1 teaspoon vanilla
1 lemon rind, finely grated
5½ cups flour

In a large bowl, mix together the sugar, butter, egg, vanilla and lemon rind until well blended. Add flour, mix gently until well blended. Do not overmix. Chill dough for at least one hour, until firm. Dust work surface with flour. Roll out dough until ¼" thick. Cut out cookies to desired shape using holiday cookie cutter. Place cookies on baking sheet pans. Bake in a preheated 375° oven until golden on top and light brown on the bottom, about 8 minutes. Makes 4 dozen cookies.

Note: Before baking, cookies can be brushed with egg wash (1 egg beaten with 1 tablespoon water and ¼ teaspoon salt) and sprinkled with colored sugar or nuts.

AAA CHOCOLATE CHIP COOKIES

2 cups butter
2 cups sugar
2 cups brown sugar
4 eggs
2 teaspoons vanilla
4 cups flour
3 cups chopped nuts

5 cups blended oatmeal*
1 teaspoon salt
2 teaspoons baking powder
2 teaspoons baking soda
4 ounces chocolate chips
1 8-ounce Hershey's
   chocolate bar grated

Cream butter and both sugars, add eggs and vanilla. In a separate bowl mix together flour, oatmeal, salt, baking powder and baking soda. Mix flour mixture with butter mixture then add chips, grated chocolate bar and nuts. Roll dough into balls and place 2" apart on a cookie sheet. Bake for 6 minutes or until golden brown. Makes 112 cookies.

*Measure oatmeal and blend in a blender to a fine powder. Recipe can be cut in half.

GRACE & ELIZA JANE'S CHOCOLATE CHIPPERS

1/2 cup unsalted butter,
   softened
3/4 cup packed light brown
   sugar
1 egg
2 tablespoons vanilla extract
3/4 cup coarsely chopped
   dates

1 cup all-purpose flour
1/2 teaspoon salt
1/2 teaspoon baking soda
1/2 teaspoon baking powder
1/4 cup grated coconut
1/2 cup granola
2 cups semi-sweet
   chocolate chips

Preheat oven to 350°. In a large bowl of an electric mixer cream the butter and brown sugar until smooth. Add the egg and vanilla and beat well. Stir in the dates and let stand for 5 minutes to soften the dates. Then beat on high speed for 3 minutes until very light brown and creamy. Combine the flour, baking soda, salt and baking powder in a bowl, breaking up any lumps; stir into creamed mixture, mixing well. Stir in the coconut, granola and chips. Drop the batter by the tablespoon onto a lightly greased cookie sheet about 1 1/2 inches apart. Bake until lightly browned, about 10-15 minutes. Immediately remove cookies from sheet and place on wire racks to cool. Store in airtight container.

A 2 Z CHOCOLATE COOKIES R YUMMY

These chocolate cookies were originally chocolate pretzels, the children love to make alphabet cookies instead.

1²/₃ cups flour
¹/₄ cup unsweetened cocoa
³/₄ cup butter or margarine, softened
³/₄ cup granulated sugar

1 teaspoon vanilla extract
1 egg white, slightly beaten
2 tablespoons coarse sugar (pearl or decorating sugar or crushed sugar cubes)

In a bowl sift together flour and cocoa to combine well; set aside. In mixer bowl combine butter and granulated sugar; beat until fluffy. Blend in vanilla. Gradually add flour mixture, beating until smooth. Gather dough into a ball and enclose in plastic wrap. Refrigerate until firm enough to shape (about 45 minutes). Preheat oven to 350°. Work with a quarter of the dough at a time, keeping remainder in refrigerator. Divide each portion into 8 equal pieces.

On a lightly floured pastry cloth or board, roll each piece into an 8" long strand using the palms of your hands. Twist each strand into a pretzel shape, or you may make alphabet letters and numbers. Place cookies about 1" apart on lightly greased baking sheets. Lightly brush each cookie with beaten egg white, then scatter coarse sugar over surface. Bake until cookies feel firm when touched lightly, 12 to 14 minutes. Let stand on baking sheets for about 2 minutes, then transfer to wire racks to cool completely. Makes 32 cookies.

PECAN CRISPIES

1 cup butter
¹/₂ cup sugar
1 teaspoon vanilla

¹/₂ cup crushed potato chips
¹/₂ cup chopped pecans
2 cups sifted flour

Preheat oven to 350°. Cream butter, sugar and vanilla. Add crushed potato chips and pecans. Stir in flour. Roll into small balls. Place on ungreased cookie sheet and press ball flat with bottom of glass dipped in sugar. Bake 15-18 minutes or until lightly brown.

PEANUT BLOSSOMS

1³/₄ cup flour
1 teaspoon baking soda
¹/₂ teaspoon salt
¹/₂ cup butter
¹/₃ cup peanut butter

¹/₂ cup sugar
¹/₂ cup brown sugar
1 egg
1 teaspoon vanilla
chocolate kisses

Preheat oven to 375°. In a small bowl mix together flour, baking soda and salt, set aside. In a large bowl, cream together butter and peanut butter; gradually add sugars, mixing thoroughly. Then add egg and vanilla; beat well. Blend in dry ingredients. Shape into 1″ balls. Roll in sugar. Place on greased baking sheet. Bake for 8 minutes, place chocolate kiss on each cookie, and bake 2-5 minutes more.

DINNY BATS

¹/₂ cup margarine
1 cup sugar
1 package pitted dates finely chopped (don't use sugar coated dates)

1 egg
1 cup chopped nuts
1 teaspoon vanilla
4 cups Rice Krispies
2 cups shredded coconut

In a large saucepan on medium heat, combine the first four ingredients stirring until dissolved. Add vanilla and nuts, continue to cook for approximately 8-10 minutes. Turn off heat. Add Rice Krispies, mix well. Shape into small balls and roll in coconut. Makes approximately 60 balls.

Food for thought: Grandma's method of restoring moisture to hardened brown sugar was to place the sugar in an airtight container together with a large apple slice.

WHITE CHOCOLATE RITZ BITZ

1 box peanut butter Ritz bits crackers
1½ pounds white chocolate

3 tablespoons shortening
decorative sprinkles

Melt white chocolate and shortening in the top of a double boiler. Dip crackers into chocolate. Put covered cracker on wax paper, decorate with sprinkles immediately. Store in air-tight container.

CHOCOLATE TURTLES

150 pecan halves (3 cups)
50 caramels

1 8-ounce package semi-sweet chocolate

Preheat oven to 300°. On greased baking sheets, arrange the pecan halves in groups of 3, flat side down, in Y shapes. Place a caramel on top of each cluster. Place in the oven until the caramels soften, about 5-8 minutes. Remove from oven and flatten the caramels over the pecans with a buttered spoon. Cool slightly. Melt the chocolate in the top of a double boiler. Dip the turtles into the chocolate and cool on wax paper. Store in tightly covered containers in a cool place.

CHOCOLATE CRACKER CANDY

40 saltine squares
1 cup brown sugar
1 cup butter

1 12-ounce package milk chocolate chips

Preheat oven to 400°. Line shallow cookie sheet with foil. Place 40 saltine squares on it (close to each other). On the stove, boil brown sugar and butter, pour and spread this over crackers. Cook crackers in oven for 5 minutes. Sprinkle chocolate chips over top of hot cracker mixture. Wait a few minutes then, as chips soften/melt spread like icing. Refrigerate. When cold, break into pieces.

PETER DOODLES

1 ½ cups creamy peanut
butter

1 12-ounce bag of
butterscotch morsels

12 ounce bag of Chinese
noodles

In double boiler or microwave, melt the butterscotch morsels.
Stir in the peanut butter and mix thoroughly. Fold in the
Chinese noodles. Place tablespoon sized mounds on cookie
sheet and refrigerate until cool.

OATRAGEOUS TOFFEE BARS

4½ cups uncooked oatmeal
1 cup packed brown sugar
¾ cup butter melted
½ cup dark corn syrup
1 teaspoon vanilla

½ teaspoon salt
1 12-ounce package
  semi-sweet chocolate chips
2 teaspoons shortening
⅔ cup chopped nuts

Preheat oven to 475°. Grease a 15 x 10" pan. Combine oats,
sugar, butter, corn syrup, vanilla and salt; mix well. Firmly
press mixture into pan. Bake 12 minutes, or until mixture is
brown and bubbly. Cool completely. In saucepan over low
heat, melt chocolate and shortening, stirring constantly until
smooth. Spread evenly over oat base; sprinkle with nuts. Chill
until set; cut into bars. Makes 60.

L.A. CHOCOLATE DECADENCE SQUARES

A chocolate lovers version of "7 layer bars". You'll find every excuse to make these rich and yummy bars.

21 Oreo sandwich cookies
4 tablespoons butter or margarine
1 ¼ cups sweetened condensed milk
1 cup semi-sweet chocolate chips

1 cup peanut butter chips
1 cup coconut flakes (optional)
1 cup coarsely chopped pecans (optional)

Preheat oven to 350°. Place the Oreos in a food processor and grind into crumbs. Place the butter in a 9 x 13″ baking pan and leave in oven until butter melts. Sprinkle Oreo crumbs over butter, stir together and press into bottom of pan, (this is the crust) Pour 1 cup sweetened condensed milk evenly over the crust. Layer chocolate chips, peanut butter chips, coconut and nuts press down firmly. Drizzle with ¼ cup condensed milk. Bake for 25-30 minutes or until lightly browned. Cool and cut into 1½″ squares. Makes 48.

RASPBERRY MERINGUE SQUARES

2½ cups flour
6 tablespoons granulated
  sugar
1 cup butter, room
  temperature but firm
5 eggs, separated
1 tablespoon vanilla extract
3½ cups raspberry jam

1 cup granulated sugar
1 tablespoon bourbon
  (or vanilla)
2 cups finely chopped
  walnuts
3 tablespoons confectioners'
  sugar

Preheat oven to 350°. In a large bowl, mix the flour and 6 tablespoons granulated sugar. With a pastry cutter or 2 knives, cut the butter into the flour mixture, tossing and mixing until the mixture resembles fine meal. With a fork or pastry blender, mix in the egg yolks and vanilla extract until blended. Press the mixture into a lightly greased 11 x 16" jelly roll pan. Bake the crust for 10 minutes or until it barely begins to brown. Remove from the oven and cool on a rack for 15 minutes. Spread the baked crust evenly with raspberry jam.

In a medium-large mixing bowl beat the egg whites until soft peaks form, add 1 cup sugar and bourbon or vanilla slowly, continuing to beat until stiff. Fold the nuts into the beaten whites and spread the mixture evenly over the raspberry. Return the pan to a 350° oven and continue baking for 30-35 minutes or until the meringue begins to brown. Remove the pan to a rack and cool completely. Dust lightly with confectioners' sugar and cut into 1½" squares.

These cookies, because they are meringue-topped, are best when served the day they are made, but may be held in an airtight tin for a few days. They are quite rich and make an excellent tea cookie.

DOMINO BARS

1 box of graham crackers (may not need all)
1 package large instant vanilla pudding
3 cups milk
1 8-ounce container Cool Whip
1 container Duncan Hines homestyle chocolate frosting (room temperature)

In a large casserole dish, layer graham crackers, set aside. In a mixing bowl combine pudding and milk, gently fold in Cool Whip. On top of graham crackers spread pudding mixture, cover with graham crackers and pudding again. Add another layer of graham crackers and spread frosting on top of this. Chill at least 5 hours. Cut into squares to serve.

ALMOND BARS

1 package of yellow cake mix
1/2 cup margarine melted
1 egg
1 teaspoon vanilla
2 eggs
8 ounces cream cheese
1 pound confectioners' sugar
4 ounces sliced almonds

Preheat oven to 350°. Combine cake mix, butter, and one egg. Beat until mixture reaches dough-like consistency. Spread into greased 9 x 13" pan. In separate bowl, combine remaining 2 eggs, vanilla, cream cheese and confectioners' sugar, beat about 3 minutes. Pour cream cheese mixture over dough mixture. Sprinkle with almonds and bake for 45 minutes. Cut when cool.

ALMOND COFFEE SLICES

1½ cups flour
¼ cup sugar
1 tablespoon instant coffee
  granules
½ cup butter, chopped

¼ cup ground almonds
1 egg, beaten
¼ cup sliced almonds
1 tablespoon sugar

Preheat oven to 350°. Sift flour in bowl; stir in sugar and coffee. Cut in butter until mixture resembles bread crumbs. Add ground almonds to form dough. Press into buttered jelly roll pan. Brush with egg and sprinkle with almonds and sugar. Bake for 20 minutes. Cool for 10 minutes, then cut into fingers.

BETTY MARTIN'S KENTUCKY FUDGE

4 tablespoons butter
4 cups sugar
1 large can evaporated milk
1 13-ounce jar of
  marshmallow cream

1 12-ounce package of
  semi-sweet chocolate chips
1 package of chopped pecans

In a saucepan combine butter, sugar, and evaporated milk, bring to a rolling boil. Boil for 9 minutes. Remove from heat. Add marshmallow, chocolate chips and pecans; mix thoroughly. Put in greased pan, let cool, and cut into squares.

Famous in four states for these ... Gayle finds a heartier welcome when handing a plate of these brownies to the host and hostess.

GAYLE'S FAMOUS BROWNIES

3/4 cup margarine, melted
1 1/2 cups sugar
1 1/2 to 2 teaspoons vanilla
3 eggs, beaten

3/4 cup all-purpose flour
1/2 cup cocoa
1/2 teaspoon baking powder
1/4 teaspoon salt

Bake at 350°. Mix all ingredients well and spread in greased 8" pan. Bake for 45 minutes. When cool, sprinkle with powdered sugar and cut into squares.

MONTESSORI BROWNIES

1 cup butter
4 tablespoons cocoa
1 cup water
2 cups flour
2 cups sugar

1/2 teaspoon salt
2 eggs
1 teaspoon soda
1/2 cup sour cream
pecans or walnuts (optional)

ICING:
1/2 cup butter
4 tablespoons cocoa
6 tablespoons milk

1 box powdered sugar
1 teaspoon vanilla

Preheat oven to 375°. In saucepan, combine butter, cocoa and water; bring to a boil. Remove from heat and pour into mixing bowl; allow to cool. To butter mixture add flour, sugar and salt, mix thoroughly. Next, beat in eggs, soda, sour cream and nuts. Pour onto greased and 11 x 16" floured cookie sheet, bake 20 to 22 minutes. While brownies are cooking, in a saucepan combine butter, cocoa, milk and bring to a boil (slightly thick). Remove from heat and add confectioners' sugar and vanilla. Spread on warm cake.

LEFTOVERS

LEFTOVERS

GINGERBREAD HOUSE DOUGH

5 cups all-purpose flour, sifted
1 teaspoon baking soda
1 teaspoon nutmeg
1 teaspoon salt
3 teaspoons powdered ginger

1 cup granulated sugar
1 cup solid vegetable white shortening (Crisco)
1 cup unsulphured molasses (like Grandma's)

In a large saucepan, over moderate heat, melt shortening in saucepan. Add granulated sugar and molasses and stir until sugar is dissolved. In a large mixing bowl, sift flour and remaining ingredients. Measure 4 cups dry ingredients from mixing bowl, reserving 1 cup, and gradually add to melted shortening mixture. Stir until blended thoroughly. Remove mixture from heat and transfer from saucepan to pastry board or countertop. Add remaining cup of dry mixture by hand. Blend thoroughly and divide the dough into three equal parts, shaping each part into a ball.

Place each ball on separate ungreased cookie sheets. With rolling pin or a straight glass bottle, roll dough into a rectangle uniformly 1/4" thick. Tip: placing a damp towel under the cookie sheets will keep them from sliding while rolling out the dough.

Cut out the part to construct your house. Bake the cut out parts right on the ungreased cookie sheets. Bake parts in preheated 375° oven for 13 to 14 minutes, or until lightly browned. All baked parts must remain on cookie sheets until completely cooled.

ICING:
2 egg whites
3 cups 10x confectioners' sugar

1 teaspoon cream of tartar (hardening agent)

Beat egg whites briefly and gradually add sugar and cream of tartar. Continue to beat until mixture reaches a smooth, creamy texture. Keep icing bowl covered with a damp towel or plastic wrap–this will delay setting of the icing.

The making of gingerbread became an art during the 15th century and reached it's height during the reign of Elizabeth I when elaborate gingerbread sculptures and molds were made for banquet guests. Guests of honor were likely greeted by a life-size gingerbread sculpture of themselves.

SIMMERING SPICE
Do not drink!

1 quart of pineapple juice	3 3" cinnamon sticks
1 quart of water	16 cloves
1 quart of apple cider	1 teaspoon allspice
4 pieces whole ginger	1-2 teaspoons pickling spice

Combine all ingredients, and heat in a crock pot or on low on the stove. Simmering spice creates a festive aroma for your home throughout the holidays.

DOGGIE DELIGHTS
Canine Cookies

2½ cups whole wheat flour	1 teaspoon granulated beef bouillon
½ cup powdered dry milk	5 tablespoons meat drippings
½ teaspoon salt	1 egg, beaten
1 teaspoon garlic powder	½ cup ice water
½ teaspoon onion powder	
2 teaspoons brown sugar	

Preheat oven to 350°. Combine first 7 ingredients. Cut in drippings until mixture resembles cornmeal. Mix in egg. Add just enough ice water to make mixture form a ball. Pat dough to ½" thick and cut into desired shapes. Place on a lightly greased cookie sheet and bake 25-30 minutes. Cool before serving. A bone shaped cookie cutter is perfect.

BIRD FOOD

1 cup peanut butter	1 cup all-purpose flour
1 cup shortening	4 cups plain cornmeal

Cream peanut butter and Crisco. Add flour and corn meal. Form into balls; large or small. Or spread onto pinecones. (The birds love it.)

"It is not true that I invented what is called the 'Montessori Method.' I have studied the child. I have taken what the child has given me and expressed it, and that is what is called the 'Montessori Method.'"
— Maria Montessori

PLAY DOUGH

1 cup flour
½ cup salt
2 teaspoons cream of tartar

1 cup water
1 tablespoon cooking oil
few drops of food coloring

Mix dry ingredients in saucepan. Add oil, water, food coloring. Cook over medium heat until the mixture pulls away from the side of the pan. A few drops of cloves or cinnamon may be added for fragrance. Knead dough slightly and store in airtight container. This play dough lasts and lasts.

FORSYTH PARK BOILED PEANUTS

3-4 pounds green peanuts, which can only be purchased in the summer

water
salt-lots of it

Put 8-9 cups of water in a 12 quart pot. Salt the water to taste. Actually, taste the water before putting in the peanuts to make sure it has the correct amount of salt for your taste, at least ⅔ cup of salt. Add all of the cleaned peanuts and bring the water to a boil. Let the peanuts simmer 1½-2 hours. Stir occasionally. When peanuts are tender, turn the heat off but let the peanuts sit at least another 2-3 hours. This allows the peanut to soak up the salt. Drain and serve warm or chilled. A great treat to take to the beach!

SPICED PECANS

1 cup sugar
½ cup water
1 teaspoon cinnamon

1 teaspoon salt
1 teaspoon vanilla
1 pound pecans

Combine sugar, water, cinnamon and salt in a saucepan. Cook on medium to 230° or threading stage. Remove from heat. Add vanilla and pecans. Stir until nuts are well coated. Pour onto a buttered platter or baking sheet. Separate nuts as they cool.

"When I was a little girl in Savannah, my father used to take us to Forsyth Park to feed the pigeons. We'd buy the peanuts from the old men in the park and eat more than we'd feed the pigeons. We also used to walk along Broughton Street to shop and there would be old women selling boiled peanuts on every corner. They were great!"

PONNIE'S CRUNCHY REFRIGERATOR PICKLES

2 quarts cucumbers from garden or farmer's market
4 onions

2 tablespoons salt
2 cups vinegar
2 cups sugar

Thinly slice the cucumbers and onions. Put sliced cucumbers and onions in colander, sprinkle with salt and let sit for 2 hours. Rinse well. In a saucepan, heat vinegar and sugar, set aside and let cool. Combine with cucumbers/onions and refrigerate for a day or two before eating.

ICED SUN TEA

"The mind is not a passive thing, but a devouring flame never in repose, always in action."
— Maria Montessori

large glass container with lid
6 small tea bags or
   2 family size tea bags

$1/2$ teaspoon baking soda

Fill container with water, add baking soda (absorbs acid in tea and keeps it from getting bitter), add tea bags. Place in a sunny spot and wait for it to finish brewing. Serve over ice with lemon, orange or a sprig of mint.

RUSSIAN TEA MIX

1 cup Tang
1 cup sugar
$1/4$ cup instant iced tea

1 teaspoon cinnamon
$1/2$ teaspoon cloves

Mix all ingredients together. Store in glass jar or container. When ready to use, add 2 teaspoons or more to each cup of boiling water. Serve hot or cold.

PINK RASPBERRY PUNCH

1 2-liter raspberry ginger ale
**1 46-ounce can pineapple
    juice**

2 quarts raspberry sherbet

Chill ginger ale and juice. Pour over raspberry sherbet. Stir gently, makes one punch bowl full. Great for baby showers!

SPICED CIDER

2 quarts apple cider
3 cinnamon sticks
40 whole cloves
1 teaspoon nutmeg

2 cups fresh orange juice
1/2 cup fresh lemon juice
2 strips orange peel

Boil cider, cinnamon, cloves and nutmeg together for 15 minutes. Add juices and orange peel. Try not to get any of the white part with the peel. Serve hot.

CLASSROOM CHRISTMAS PUNCH

Serves 50-100

**3-4 large bottles cranberry
    juice**
**2-3 large cans pineapple
    juice**

3 quarts ginger ale
**1-3 teaspoons almond extract
    to taste**
ice

Combine ingredients in order listed. Can be reduced in thirds/ratio of 1-1-1-1. Use a tad less pineapple juice than cranberry juice.

SNUGGLE UP HOT COCOA MIX

**1 cup powdered nondairy
    coffee creamer**
1 cup sifted powdered sugar
1/4 cup cocoa

**1/4 cup mint chocolate
    morsels**
**1/2 cup miniature
    marshmallows**

Combine all ingredients; store in an airtight container. Makes 2 1/3 cups mix. Directions for gift recipe card: Add 2/3 cup boiling water to 1/3 cup Hot Cocoa Mix. Enjoy hot, soothing mug of cocoa.

SCHRAFFT'S CHOCOLATE FUDGE SAUCE

2 squares bittersweet
   chocolate
2 tablespoons butter
1/3 cup boiling water

1 cup sugar
2 tablespoons Karo
   light corn syrup
1 teaspoon vanilla

In a saucepan stir the chocolate and butter on low heat until completely melted. Then add the water, sugar and syrup, bring to a boil. Boil for 4 to 5, minutes then add vanilla. Serve warm over anything!

SINFULLY GOOD CHOCOLATE SAUCE

1 can Hershey's chocolate
   syrup
1 can sweetened condensed
   milk

1 stick butter

Melt butter in saucepan. Add chocolate syrup and sweetened condensed milk. Mix and stir just before boiling. Serve over ice cream, pound cake, brownies, strawberries, etc. Store leftover sauce in refrigerator.

BUTTERMILK SAUCE

1 cup sugar
1/2 cup butter
1/2 cup buttermilk
1 tablespoon white Karo
   syrup

1/2 teaspoon baking soda
1 teaspoon vanilla

Combine sugar, butter, buttermilk, Karo and baking soda in sauce pan. Heat to almost boiling, add vanilla, stir and serve. Great over angel food cake, fresh fruit, ice cream or brownies. (Or grab a spoon and eat it right out of the jar!) Buttermilk sauce keeps when stored in airtight container in the refrigerator for at least 2-4 months.

"Free the child's potential and you will transform him and the world."
— Maria Montessori

TEDDY'S BREAKFAST BEAR SPREAD

1 cup lowfat or nonfat plain yogurt
1 tablespoon cinnamon (to taste)

1 tablespoon honey (to taste)

The night before, scoop plain yogurt into strainer. Don't forget the bowl for it to strain into. In the morning empty yogurt into small bowl. Have Teddy add lotsa cinnamon and a smackerel of honey. Sing together, "Isn't it funny how a bear loves honey," Stirrryummmmy! Toast up your favorite bagel, bread and spread. Lots of protein, low on fat.

Variation: With strained yogurt add huge clove of crushed garlic, fresh ground pepper and freshly chopped herbs (dill, basil etc.). Makes a great appetizer dip.

This recipe calls for a yogurt strainer, a useful inexpensive item sold at kitchen specialty shops.

JEZEBEL SAUCE

18 ounces pineapple preserves
18 ounces apple jelly
5 ounces good quality horseradish

¼ cup dry mustard
cracked black pepper

In a large bowl, toss together all the ingredients. Mix the daylights out of it with a wire whisk, taking care to break up the blobs of apple jelly. Serve as a condiment with any meat, especially roast beef and turkey. Can be spooned over block of cream cheese and served with crackers. Will keep indefinitely in the fridge. Double the recipe and spoon into small decorative jars. Makes a unique gift for the holidays.

CRANBERRY SAUCE

1 pound fresh cranberries
1 apple, peeled, cored and chopped (Granny Smith's are good)
2 large oranges, peeled and chopped

$^3/_4$ cup sugar
$^1/_2$ cup water
juice of one juicy lemon

Combine all ingredients in a heavy saucepan. Cover and cook over very low heat, stirring occasionally, for 3 or 4 hours. Serve hot or cold. Great on leftover turkey sandwiches. Makes 3 cups. Smells terrific.

MANGO SALSA

2 ripe medium sized mangos
1 small cucumber, peeled seeded and diced
1 ripe tomato chopped
juice of one lime

dash of salt
dash of Tabasco
1 tablespoon fresh cilantro chopped

Peel and chop the mangos. In a large bowl, combine the mangos, cucumber, tomato, lime juice, salt, Tabasco and cilantro. Let the mixture stand for about 10 minutes to let the flavors blend. Refrigerate. Keeps for 2-3 days.

PESTO

3 cups loosely packed fresh basil leaves
$^1/_3$ cup pine nuts
$^1/_2$ cup grated Parmesan cheese

3 garlic cloves, coarsely chopped
$^1/_2$ cup olive oil
salt and ground black pepper to taste

In a food processor or blender combine all ingredients except oil. When well chopped, add the oil in a thin stream to form a smooth paste. Pesto will keep refrigerated for 1 week. If freezing pesto, store in plastic bags or in ice cube trays. Whirl frozen thawed pesto in the blender briefly to improve it's texture.

MOLASSES MARINADE FOR CHICKEN OR PORK

1/2 cup soy sauce
1/4 cup salad oil
2 tablespoons molasses
2 teaspoons ground ginger
2 teaspoons dry mustard

6 cloves garlic minced
8 pieces boneless chicken
 or other chicken pieces,
 or 1 or 2 pork tenderloins

Mix all ingredients together. Add chicken or pork and marinate for one hour or several hours, the longer the better. Grill over hot coals. Marinate fresh pineapple slices while meat cooks. Grill pineapple for a few minutes and place on top of chicken.

HOMEMADE MAYO

1 teaspoon paprika
1/4 teaspoon salt
1 teaspoon powdered
 mustard
1 pinch oregano

2 tablespoons of lemon juice
2 tablespoons of tarragon
 vinegar
1 1/2 cups Wesson oil

Blend all ingredients except oil in mixer. Slowly add oil. Refrigerate.

CLEMSON BLUE CHEESE DRESSING

6 ounces Clemson blue
 cheese
1 small can evaporated milk,
 chilled and whipped

1 3/4 cup mayonnaise
juice of 1/2 a lemon
garlic salt

Mix all ingredients with hand mixer. Chill several hours. Stir and eat with potato chips or use as salad dressing.

HERB VINAIGRETTE WITH HERB CHEESE CROUTONS

1/2 cup olive oil	1 teaspoon dried Italian
1/2 cup vegetable oil	seasoning
1/3-1/2 cup white wine vinegar	1/2 teaspoon freshly ground
3 tablespoons grated	pepper
Parmesan cheese	1/2 teaspoon dried parsley
1 1/2 tablespoons Dijon	flakes
mustard	1 clove garlic, crushed

Combine all ingredients in container of an electric blender; process until smooth, stopping once to scrape down sides. Store in refrigerator up to 3 months. Yield 1 1/2 cups.

CROUTONS:

1 13-ounce package small	1/4 cup grated Parmesan
soft breadsticks	cheese
1/4 cup olive oil	2 teaspoons dried Italian
1/4 cup butter or margarine,	seasoning
melted	1/4 teaspoon pepper
2 cloves garlic, minced	

Preheat oven to 400°. Slice bread with a serrated knife into 3/8" thick rounds. Combine olive oil, butter and garlic; drizzle over bread rounds, tossing to coat. Combine Parmesan cheese, Italian seasoning, and red pepper; sprinkle over bread rounds, tossing to coat. Place on baking sheet; bake for 5 minutes. Turn rounds over and bake an additional 2 to 5 minutes or until crisp and golden brown. Cool and store in an airtight container for up to 3 weeks. Yield: 10 cups.

INDEX

INDEX

INDEX

Mail to: Sea Pines Montessori School Cookbook
9 Fox Grape Road
Hilton Head Island, SC 29928 • 803-785-2534

Please send me_____copies @ $16.95 each $_____

Plus Postage & Handling $3.50 each $_____

SC residents please add sales tax .85¢ each $_____

Please gift wrap @ $1.00 per book $1.00 each $_____

Total $_____

Please make checks payable to: Sea Pines Montessori School Cookbook

Name_____

Address_____

City/State/Zip_____

- -

Mail to: Sea Pines Montessori School Cookbook
9 Fox Grape Road
Hilton Head Island, SC 29928 • 803-785-2534

Please send me_____copies @ $16.95 each $_____

Plus Postage & Handling $3.50 each $_____

SC residents please add sales tax .85¢ each $_____

Please gift wrap @ $1.00 per book $1.00 each $_____

Total $_____

Please make checks payable to: Sea Pines Montessori School Cookbook

Name_____

Address_____

City/State/Zip_____

- -

Mail to: Sea Pines Montessori School Cookbook
9 Fox Grape Road
Hilton Head Island, SC 29928 • 803-785-2534

Please send me_____copies @ $16.95 each $_____

Plus Postage & Handling $3.50 each $_____

SC residents please add sales tax .85¢ each $_____

Please gift wrap @ $1.00 per book $1.00 each $_____

Total $_____

Please make checks payable to: Sea Pines Montessori School Cookbook

Name_____

Address_____

City/State/Zip_____

The Sea Pines Montessori School does not discriminate on the basis of race, color, creed, sex, national or ethnic origin, in the administration of its educational policies, admissions policies, financial aid programs, and all other school administered programs.